A View of Society aı

France, Switzerland, and Germany

Vol. 2

With Anecdotes Relating to Some

Eminent Characters

John Moore

Alpha Editions

This edition published in 2024

ISBN : 9789362927187

Design and Setting By
Alpha Editions
www.alphaedis.com
Email - info@alphaedis.com

Contents

LETTER L.

DEAR SIR,

Since my return from Darmstadt, the weather has been so very bad, that I have passed the time mostly at home. That I may obey your injunctions to write regularly at the stated periods, I will send you the substance of a conversation I had within these few days with a foreigner, a man of letters, with whom I am in a considerable degree of intimacy.

This gentleman has never been in England, but he speaks the language a little, understands it very well, and has studied many of our best Authors. He said, that he had found in some English books, a solidity of reasoning, and a strength of expression, superior to any thing he had met with elsewhere;— that the English history furnished examples of patriotism and zeal for civil liberty, equal to what was recorded in the Greek or Roman story;—that English poetry displayed a sublimity of thought, and a knowledge of the human heart, which no writings, ancient or modern, could surpass; and in philosophy it was pretty generally allowed, that the English nation had no rival.—He then mentioned the improvements made by Englishmen in medicine and other arts, their superiority in navigation, commerce, and manufactures; and even hinted something in praise of a few English statesmen. He concluded his panegyric by saying, that these considerations had given him the highest idea of the English nation, and had led him to cultivate the acquaintance of many Englishmen whom he had occasionally met on their travels. But he frankly acknowledged, that his connection with these had not contributed to support the idea he had formed of their nation.

As I had heard sentiments of the same kind insinuated by others, I replied at some length, observing, that if he had lived in the most brilliant period of Roman grandeur, and had accidentally met with a few Romans in Greece or Asia, and had formed his opinion of that illustrious commonwealth from the conduct and conversation of these travellers, his ideas would, in all probability, have been very different from those which the writings of Livy, Cæsar, Cicero, and Virgil, had given him of the Roman people:—That the manners and behaviour of the few English he might have met abroad, so far from giving him a just view of the character of the whole nation, very possibly had led him to false conclusions with regard to the character of those very individuals. For that I myself had known many young Englishmen who, after having led a dissipated, insignificant kind of life while on their travels, and while the natural objects of their ambition were at a distance, had changed their conduct entirely upon their return, applied to business as eagerly as they had formerly launched into extravagance, and had at length become very useful members of the community.

But, continued I, throwing this consideration out of the question, the real character of a people can only be discovered by living among them on a familiar footing, and for a considerable time. This is necessary before we can form a just idea of any nation; but perhaps more so with respect to the English, than any other: for in no nation are the education, sentiments, and pursuits of those who travel, so different from those of the people who remain at home.

The first class is composed of a few invalids, a great many young men raw from the university, and some idle men of fortune, void of ambition, and incapable of application, who, every now and then, saunter through Europe, because they know not how to employ their time at home.

The second class is made up of younger brothers, who are bred to the army, navy, the law, and other professions;—all who follow commerce, are employed in manufactures, or farming;—and, in one word, all who, not being born to independent fortunes, endeavour to remedy that inconveniency by industry, and the cultivation of their talents.

England is the only country in Europe whose inhabitants never leave it in search of fortune. There are, moderately speaking, twenty Frenchmen in London for every Englishman at Paris. By far the greater part of those Frenchmen travel to get money, and almost all the English to spend it. But we should certainly be led into great errors, by forming an idea of the character of the French nation from that of the French fiddlers, dancing-masters, dentists, and valet-de-chambres to be met with in England, or other parts of Europe.

The gentleman acknowledged, that it would be unfair to decide on the French character from that of their fiddlers and dancing-masters; but added, that he did not perceive that the English could reasonably complain, should foreigners form an opinion of their national character from the men of fortune, rank, and the most liberal education of their island.

I answered, they certainly would, because young men of high rank and great fortune carry a set of ideas along with them from their infancy, which very often disappoint the purposes of the best education.—— Let a child of high rank be brought up with all the care and attention the most judicious parents and matters can give;—let him be told, that personal qualities alone can make him truly respectable;—that the fortuitous circumstances of birth and fortune afford no just foundation for esteem;—that knowledge and virtue are the true sources of honour and happiness;—that idleness produces vice and misery;—that without application he cannot acquire knowledge;—and that without knowledge he will dwindle into insignificance, in spite of rank and fortune:—— Let these things be inculcated with all the power of persuasion; let them be illustrated by example, and insinuated by fable and allegory;—yet, do we not daily see the effect of all this counteracted by the insinuations of servants and base sycophants, who give an importance to far different qualities, and preach a much more agreeable doctrine?——

They make eternal allusions in all their discourse and behaviour to the great estate the young spark is one day to have, and the great man he must be, independent of any effort of his own. They plainly insinuate, if they do not directly say it, that study and application, tho' proper enough for hospital boys, is unnecessary, or perhaps unbecoming a man of fashion. They talk with rapture of the hounds, hunters, and race-horses of one great man; of the rich liveries and brilliant equipage of another; and how much both are loved and admired for their liberality to their servants. They tell their young master, that his rank and estate entitle him to have finer hounds, horses, liveries and equipage than either, and to be more liberal to his servants; and consequently a greater man in every respect. This kind of poison, being often poured upon the young sprouts of fortune and quality, gradually blasts the vigour of the plants, and renders all care and cultivation ineffectual.

If we suppose that domestics of another character could be placed about a boy of high rank, and every measure taken to inspire him with other sentiments; he cannot stir abroad, he cannot go into company without perceiving his own importance, and the attention that is paid to him. His childish pranks are called spirited actions; his pert speeches are converted into bon mots; and when reproved or punished by his parent or master, ten to one but some obsequious intermeddler will tell him that he has suffered great injustice.

The youth, improving all this to the purposes of indolence and vanity, arrives at length at the comfortable persuasion, that study or application of any kind would in him be superfluous;—that he ought only to seek amusement, for at the blessed age of twenty-one, distinction, deference, admiration, and all other good things will be added unto him.

A young man, on the other hand, who is born to no such expectations, has no sycophants around him to pervert his understanding;—when he behaves improperly, he instantly sees the marks of disapprobation on every countenance:—He daily meets with people who inform him of his faults without ceremony or circumlocution.—He perceives that nobody cares for his bad humour or caprice, and very naturally concludes that he had best correct his temper.—He finds that he is apt to be neglected in company, and that the only remedy for this inconveniency will be the rendering himself agreeable.—He loves affluence, distinction, and admiration, as well as the rich and great; but becomes fully convinced that he can never obtain even the shadow of them, otherwise than by useful and ornamental acquirements. The truth of those precepts, which is proved by rhetoric and syllogism to the boy of fortune, is experimentally felt by him who has no fortune; and the difference which this makes, is infinite.

So that the son of a gentleman of moderate fortune has a probability of knowing more of the world at the age of sixteen, and of having a juster notion of people's sentiments of him, than a youth of very high rank at a much more advanced age; for it is very difficult for any person to find out that he is despised while he continues to be flattered.

So far, therefore, from being surprised that dissipation, weakness and ignorance, are so prevalent among those who are born to great fortunes and high rank, we ought to be astonished to see so great a number of men of virtue, diligence and genius among them as there is. And if the number be proportionably greater in England than in any other country, which I believe is the case, this must proceed from the impartial discipline of our public schools; and the equitable treatment which boys of the greatest rank receive from their comrades. Sometimes the natural, manly sentiments they acquire from their school companions, serve as an antidote against the childish, sophistical notions with which weak or designing men endeavour to inspire them in after-life.

The nature of the British constitution contributes also to form a greater number of men of talents among the wealthy and the great, than are to be found in other countries; because it opens a wider field for ambition than any other government;—and ambition excites those exertions which produce talents.

But, continued I, you must acknowledge that it would be improper to form a judgment of the English genius, by samples taken from men who have greater temptations to indolence, and fewer spurs to application than others.

My disputant still contested the point, and asserted that high birth gave a native dignity and elevation to the mind;—that distinctions and honours were originally introduced into families by eminent abilities and great virtues;—that when a man of illustrious birth came into a company, or even when his name was mentioned, this naturally raised a recollection of the great actions and shining qualities of the eminent person who had first acquired those honours;—that a consciousness of this must naturally stimulate the present possessor to imitate the virtues of his ancestors;—that his degenerating would subject him to the highest degree of censure, as the world could not, without indignation, behold indolence and vice adorned with the rewards of activity and virtue.

I might have disputed this assertion, that honours and titles are always the rewards of virtue; and could have produced abundance of instances of the opposite proposition. But I allowed that they often were so, and that hereditary honours in a family always ought to have, and sometimes had, the effect which he supposed: but these concessions being made in their fullest extent, still he would do injustice to the English, by forming a judgment of their national character from what he had observed of the temper, manners, and genius of those Englishmen with whom he had been acquainted in foreign countries; because three-fourths of them were, in all probability, men of fortune, without having family or high birth to boast of; so that they had the greatest inducements to indolence, without possessing the motives to virtuous exertions, which influence people of high rank.—For, though it rarely happened in other countries, it was very common in England for men of all the various professions and trades to accumulate very great fortunes, which, at their death, falling to their sons, these young men, without having had a suitable education, immediately set up for gentlemen, and run over Europe in the characters of Milords Anglois, game, purchase pictures, mutilated statues and mistresses, to the astonishment of all beholders: And, conscious of the blot in their escutcheon, they think it is incumbent on them to wash it out, and make up for the impurity of their blood, by plunging deeper into the ocean of extravagance than is necessary for a man of hereditary fashion.

Here our conversation ended, and the gentleman promised that he would abide by the idea he had formed of the English nation from the works of Milton, Locke and Newton, and the characters of Raleigh, Hambden, and Sidney.

LETTER LI.

Among the remarkable things in Frankfort the inns may be reckoned. Two in particular, the Emperor and the Red House, for cleanliness, conveniency, and number of apartments, are superior to any I ever saw on the continent, and vie with our most magnificent inns in England.

At these, as at all other inns in Germany and Switzerland, there is an ordinary, at which the strangers may dine and sup. This is called the Table d'Hôte, from the circumstance of the landlord's sitting at the bottom of the table and carving the victuals. The same name for an ordinary is still retained in France, tho' the landlord does not sit at the table, which was the case formerly in that country, and still is the custom in Germany.

There are no private lodgings to be had here as in London, nor any hôtels garnis as in Paris. Strangers therefore retain apartments at the inn during the whole time of their residence in any of the towns. And travellers of every denomination in this country under the rank of sovereign princes, make no scruple of eating occasionally at the table d'Hôte of the inn where they lodge, which custom is universally followed by strangers from every country on the continent of Europe.

Many of our countrymen, however, who despise œconomy, and hate the company of strangers, prefer eating in their own apartments to the table d'Hôte, or any private table to which they may be invited.

It would be arrogance in any body to dispute the right which every free-born Englishman has to follow his own inclination in this particular: Yet when people wish to avoid the company of strangers, it strikes me, that they might indulge their fancy as completely at home as abroad; and while they continue in that humour, I cannot help thinking that they might save themselves the inconveniency and expence of travelling.

The manners and genius of nations, it is true, are not to be learnt at inns; nor is the most select company to be found at public ordinaries; yet a person of observation, and who is fond of the study of character, will sometimes find instruction and entertainment at both. He there sees the inhabitants of the country on a less ceremonious footing than he can elsewhere, and hears the remarks of travellers of every degree.

The first care of a traveller certainly should be, to form an acquaintance and some degree of intimacy with the principal people in every place where he intends to reside;—to accept invitations to their family parties, and attend their societies;—to entertain them at his apartments, when that can be conveniently done, and endeavour to acquire a just notion of their government, customs, sentiments, and manner of living.—Those who are fond of the study of man, which, with all due deference to the philosophers who prefer that of beasts, birds and butterflies, is also a pardonable amusement, will mix occasionally with all degrees of people, and, when not otherwise engaged, will not scruple to take a seat at the table d'Hôte.

It is said that low people are sometimes to be found at these ordinaries. This to be sure is a weighty objection; but then it should be remembered, that it is within the bounds of possibility that men even engaged in commerce, may have liberal minds, and may be able to give as distinct accounts of what is worthy of observation, as if they had been as idle as people of the highest fashion through the whole of their lives. A man must have a very turgid idea of his own grandeur, if he cannot submit, in a foreign country, to dine at table with a person of inferior rank; especially as he will meet, at the same time, with others of equal, or superior rank to himself: For all etiquette of this nature is waved even in Germany at the tables d'Hôtes.

A knowledge of the characters of men, as they appear varied in different situations and countries;—the study of human nature indeed in all its forms and modifications, is highly interesting to the mind, and worthy the attention of the greatest man. This is not to be perfectly attained in courts and palaces. The investigator of nature must visit her in humbler life, and put himself on a level with the men whom he wishes to know.

It is generally found, that those who possess real greatness of mind, never hesitate to overleap the obstacles, and despise the forms, which may stand in the way of their acquiring this useful knowledge.

The most powerful of all arguments against entirely declining to appear at the public table of the inn, is, that in this country it is customary for the ladies themselves, when on a journey, to eat there; and my partiality for the table d'Hôte may possibly be owing in some degree to my having met, at one of them, with two of the handsomest women that I have seen since I have been in this country, which abounds in female beauty.

There is more expression in the countenances of French women, but the ladies in Germany have the advantage in the fairness of their skin and the bloom of their complexion. They have a greater resemblance to English women than to French; yet they differ considerably from them both.—I do not know how to give an idea of the various shades of expression, which, if

I mistake not, I can distinguish in the features of the sex in these three countries.

A handsome French woman, besides the ease of her manner, has commonly a look of cheerfulness and great vivacity.—She appears willing to be acquainted with you, and seems to expect that you should address her.

The manner of an English woman is not so devoid of restraint; and a stranger, especially if he be a foreigner, may observe a look which borders on disdain in her countenance. Even among the loveliest features, something of a sulky air often appears. While their beauty allures, this in some degree checks that freedom of address which you might use to the Frenchwoman, and interests your vanity more, by giving the idea of the difficulties you have to conquer.

A German beauty, without the smart air of the one, or the reserve of the other, has generally a more placid look than either.

LETTER LII.

Several individuals here are fond of distinguishing themselves by their passion for the fine arts, and strangers are informed, that it is well worth while to visit certain private collections of paintings which are to be seen at Frankfort.

You know I am no connoisseur; and if I were, should not take up your time in describing them, or giving a criticism on their subject. For though I have seen them, you have not; and nothing, in my opinion, can be more unintelligible and tiresome to the Reader, than criticisms on paintings which he has not seen. I shall only observe, that as all these collections have acquired the esteem and approbation of the proprietors, which I presume was the chief end of their creation, they are certainly intitled to respect from every unconcerned spectator.—— One of them in particular must be very valuable, on account of the prodigious sum of money which the present possessor was offered for it, and which he refused as inadequate to its worth; though the sum offered would have at once made the gentleman easy in his circumstances, which, I am sorry to say, is far from being the case. This anecdote cannot be doubted, for I had it from his own mouth.

It is still more the fashion here to form cabinets of natural curiosities. Besides the repositories of this kind, which are to be seen at the courts of the princes, many individuals all over Germany have Museums in their houses, and strangers cannot pay their court better, than by requesting permission to see them. This would be an easy piece of politeness, if the stranger were allowed to take a view, and walk away when he thought proper. But the misfortune is, that the proprietor attends on these occasions, and gives the history of every piece of ore, petrifaction, fossil-wood, and monster that is in the collection. And as this lecture is given gratis, he assumes the right of making it as long as he pleases: so that requesting a sight of a private collection of natural curiosities, is a more serious matter than people are aware of.

The D—— of H—— has brought himself into a scrape, out of which I imagine it will be difficult to extricate him. Being unacquainted with the trouble which these gentlemen give themselves on such occasions, he has expressed an inclination to three or four virtuosi to see their cabinets. I attended him on his first visitation yesterday. The gentleman made an unusual exertion to please his Grace. He said, being fully convinced of his taste for natural philosophy, in which people of his high rank were never deficient, he would therefore take pleasure to explain every particular in the collection with the greatest deliberation. He had kept himself disengaged the whole forenoon on purpose, and had given orders not to be interrupted. He then descanted on each particular in the collection, with such minuteness and perseverance, as completely satiated His Grace's curiosity, and gave him such a knowledge of earths, crystals, agates, pyrites, marcasites, petrifactions, metals, semi-metals, &c. &c. as will, I dare swear, serve him for the rest of his life.

Cassel.

I began this letter at Frankfort, not suspecting that our departure would be so sudden. But as the day approached on which we had been promised the sight of another cabinet of curiosities, I found the D——'s impatience to be gone increase every moment. So sending our apology to the proprietors of two or three which he had asked permission to visit, we passed one day with Madame de Barkhause's family, and another with Mr. Gogle's, and then bidding a hasty adieu to our other acquaintances at Frankfort, we set out for this place. We slept the first night at Marburg, and on the second, about midnight, arrived at Cassel.

As the ground is quite covered with snow, the roads bad, and the posts long, we were obliged to take six horses for each chaise, which, after all, in some places moved no faster than a couple of hearses. The D—— bore this with wonderful serenity, contemplating the happy evasion he had made from the cabinets at Frankfort. A slave who had escaped from the mines could not have shown greater satisfaction. His good humour remained proof against all the phlegm and obstinacy of the German postillions, of which one who has not travelled in the extremity of the winter, and when the roads are covered with snow, through this country, can form no idea.

The contrast of character between the French and Germans is strongly illustrated in the behaviour of the postillions of the two countries.

A French postillion is generally either laughing, or fretting, or singing, or swearing, all the time he is on the road. If a hill or a bad road oblige him to go slow, he will of a sudden fall a cracking his whip above his head for a quarter of an hour together, without rhyme or reason; for he knows the horses cannot go a bit faster, and he does not intend they should. All this noise and emotion, therefore, means nothing; and proceeds entirely from that abhorrence of quiet which every Frenchman sucks in with his mother's milk.

A German postillion, on the contrary, drives four horses with all possible tranquillity. He neither sings, nor frets, nor laughs: he only smokes;—and when he comes near a narrow defile, he sounds his trumpet to prevent any carriage from entering at the other end till he has got through. If you call to him to go faster, he turns about, looks you in the face, takes his pipe from his mouth, and says, Yaw, Mynher;—yaw, yaw; and then proceeds exactly in the same pace as before. He is no way affected whether the road be good or bad; whether it rains, or shines, or snows:—And he seems to be totally regardless of the people whom he drives, and equally callous to their reproach or applause. He has one object of which he never loses sight, which is, to conduct your chaise and the contents from one post to another, in the manner he thinks best for himself and the horses. And unless his pipe goes out (in which case he strikes his flint and rekindles it), he seems not to have another idea during the whole journey.

Your best course is to let him take his own way at first, for it will come to that at last.—All your noise and bluster are vain.

Non vultus instantis tyranni

Mente quatit solida, neque Auster

Dux inquieti turbidus Adriæ,

Nec fulminantis magna Jovis manus.

LETTER LIII.

Cassel.

The attention and civilities which are paid to the D—— of H—— by this court, have induced us to remain longer than we intended at our arrival.

As you seem curious to know how we pass our time, and the style of living here, I shall give you a sketch of one day, which, with little variation, may give you an idea of all the rest.

We generally employ the morning and forenoon in study. We go to the palace about half an hour before dinner is served, where we find all the officers who have been invited, assembled in a large room. The Landgrave soon appears, and continues conversing with the company till his consort arrives with the princess Charlotte, and such ladies as they have thought proper to invite.

The company then walk to the dining parlour, where there are about thirty covers every day, and the same number in a room adjoining. The doors being left open between these apartments, the whole forms in a manner but one company. The strangers, and such officers as are not under the rank of colonel, dine at their Highnesses table.

The repast continues about two hours, during which the conversation is carried on with some little appearance of constraint, and rather in a low voice, except when either of their Highnesses speaks to any person seated at a little distance.

After dinner the company returns to the room where they first assembled. In this they remain till the Landgrave retires, which he usually does within about a quarter of an hour. Soon after the company separates till seven in the evening, when they again assemble.

The Landgrave plays constantly at Cavaniolle, a kind of lottery, where no address or attention is requisite, and which needs hardly interrupt conversation. It requires about a dozen players to make his party.

The Landgravine plays at Quadrille, and chooses her own party every night.—Other card-tables are set in the adjoining rooms, for the conveniency of any who choose to play. The gaming continues about a couple of hours. The Landgrave then salutes her Highness on both cheeks, and retires to his own apartments, while she and the rest of the company go to supper. At this repast there is less formality, and of consequence more ease and gaiety, than at dinner.

When her Highness rises from table, most part of the company attend her up stairs to a spacious anti-chamber, where she remains conversing a few minutes, and then retires.

These general forms are sometimes varied by a concert in the Landgrave's apartments. There are also certain days of Gala, which are only distinguished by the company's being more numerous, and better dressed, than usual: two circumstances which do not add a vast deal to the pleasure of the entertainment.

During the Carnival, there were two or three masquerades. On these occasions the court assemble about six in the evening, the men being all in Dominos, and the ladies in their usual dress, or with the addition of a few fanciful ornaments, according to the particular taste of each.

They amuse themselves with cards and conversation till the hour of supper. During this interval, a gentleman of the court carries a parcel of tickets in his hat, equal to the number of men in company. These are presented to the ladies, each of whom draws one. Tickets in the same manner are presented to the men, who take one a-piece, which they keep till the card-playing is finished.

The officer then calls number One, upon which the couple who are possessed of that number come forward, and the gentleman leads the lady into the supper-room, sits by her, and is her partner for the rest of the evening. In the same manner every other Number is called.

After supper, all the company put on their masks. Her Highness is led into the masquerade room. The rest follow, each lady being handed by her partner. The Landgravine and her partner walk to the upper end of the room.—The next couple stop at a small distance below them;—the third, next to the second, and so on till this double file reaches from the top to the bottom of the hall. If there are any supernumeraries, they must retire to the sides.—From this arrangement you expect a country dance:—a minuet however is intended—the music begins, and all the maskers on the floor, consisting of twenty or thirty couple, walk a minuet together. This, which is rather a confused affair, being over, every body sits down, the Landgravine excepted, who generally dances nine or ten minuets successively with as many different gentlemen. She then takes her seat till the rest of the company have danced minuets, which being over, the cotillons and country-dances begin, and continue till four or five in the morning.

Her Highness is a very beautiful woman, graceful in her person, and of a gay and sprightly character. She is in danger of growing corpulent, an inconveniency not uncommon in Germany, but which she endeavours to retard by using a great deal of exercise.

Besides the company who sup at court, the rooms were generally crowded with masks from the town, some of whom are in fancy-dresses, and keep themselves concealed all the time. And although those who came from the court are known when they enter the masquerade rooms, many of them slip out afterwards, change their dress, and return to amuse themselves, by teasing their friends in their assumed characters, as is usual at masquerades.

The country-dances are composed of all persons promiscuously, who incline to join in them.—Two women of pleasure, who had come to pass the Carnival at Cassel in the exercise of their profession, and were well known to many of the officers, danced every masquerade night in the country-dance, which her Highness led down; for the mask annihilates ceremony, puts every body on a footing, and not unfrequently, while it conceals the face most effectually, serves so much the more to discover the real character and inclinations of the wearer.

LETTER LIV.

Next to the Electors of the Empire, the Landgrave of Hesse Cassel is one of the greatest Princes in Germany; and even of those, the electors of Bohemia, Bavaria, Saxony, and Hanover, only are richer and more powerful than he. His country is in general hilly, with a great deal of wood, but interspersed with fertile vallies and corn-fields. The large subsidies this court received from Britain during the two last wars, with what is given in the time of peace, by way of retaining fee, have greatly contributed to the present flourishing state of its finances.

The reigning Prince forsook the Protestant faith about twenty years ago, and made a public profession of the Roman Catholic religion, in the lifetime of the late Landgrave, his father. This gave great uneasiness to the old Prince, and alarmed his subjects, who are all Protestants.

The states of the Landgraviate were assembled on this important occasion, and such measures taken as were judged necessary to maintain the religion and constitution of the country, against any future attempt to subvert them. The Hereditary Prince was excluded from all share in the education of his sons, who were put under the tuition of the Princess Mary of Great Britain, his first wife, living at that time separate from her husband. The eldest son, upon his father's accession to the Landgraviate, was put in possession of the county of Hanau; so that the inhabitants have felt no inconveniency from the change of their Prince's religion. And as he himself has reaped no earthly advantage, either in point of honour or profit, by his conversion, it is presumable, that his Highness's hopes are now limited to the rewards which may await him in another world.

This Prince keeps on foot 16000, men in time of peace, disciplined according to the Prussian plan, the Landgrave himself having the rank of Field Marshal in the Prussian army. The Prince is fond of exercising them; but not having a house on purpose, as the Prince of Hesse Darmstadt has, he takes that amusement when, the weather is very bad in the dining-room of his palace, where I have frequently seen two or three hundred of the first battalion of guards perform their manœuvres with all possible dexterity.

The Prince of Saxe-Gotha, brother to the late Princess of Wales, has a regiment in the Landgrave's service, and resides at Cassel.

The person who has the chief management in military affairs, is General Scliven, a man of an exceeding just and accurate understanding, which he has finely cultivated by reading and reflection.

I have the happiness to be intimately acquainted with many other officers in this service.—An open manner, and undesigning civility, distinguish the German character; qualities which naturally banish reserve, and inspire confidence. And what makes the conversation of these gentlemen still more agreeable and interesting to me, is the justice they seem fond of rendering to the bravery of the British troops with whom they served. They always mention the names of Granby, Waldgrave, and Kingsley, with the highest encomiums, and speak with affectionate regard of some officers with whom they were more intimately acquainted, particularly Mr. Keith, now at Vienna, and Colonel John Maxwell, whom they applaud as one of the bravest and most active officers that served in the allied army; and seem fond of mentioning instances of the amazing intrepidity of the British grenadiers whom he commanded.

Besides those actually in the Landgrave's service, there are some other persons of note who reside at Cassel. I sometimes pass an afternoon with old General Zastrow, who had the command of the garrison of Schweidnitz, when it was surprised by the Austrian general Laudohn.

If you recollect, that important place had been taken from the Prussians in the year 1757, by Count Nadasti. It was blockaded by the King of Prussia in the winter of that same year, and surrendered to him in spring 1758, after one half of the garrison had fallen in defending the place. In the year 1761, Laudohn retook it almost in sight of the Prussian monarchy by the most brilliant coup-de-main that perhaps ever was struck.

The King's army and Laudohn's were both in the neighbourhood of Schweidnitz. The latter could not attempt a regular siege, while he was watched by such an enterprising enemy. But observing that the King had moved at a greater distance than usual from the town, and knowing that more than one half of the garrison had been drafted, he resolved on an enterprise as bold as it was sagacious. One morning early this vigilant commander, taking the advantage of a thick fog, marched his army to the town, of Schweidnitz in four divisions. Scaling-ladders were applied to the ramparts, and some of the Austrians had actually entered the town, before they were observed by the centinels.

The garrison, being at last roused, attacked the assailants in a furious manner.—The confusion was increased by the blowing up of a powder magazine, which destroyed great numbers on both sides. The Governor was taken prisoner, fighting sword in hand on the ramparts, and the town surrendered.

This exploit established the reputation of Laudohn, while poor Zastrow, according to the usual fate of the unfortunate, became a prey to the calumny of the unfeeling and ungenerous. He demanded a trial by a court martial.—The King said there was no occasion for that, as he did not accuse him of any crime.—But he did not judge it expedient to employ him in any command after this misfortune.

I have heard the old man relate all the particulars of that affair, and the account he gave has been confirmed to me by officers well informed, and unconnected with him.

A company of French comedians are lately arrived here, which forms a new resource for the court. They remain six weeks, or two months. The Landgrave pays them a stipulated sum for acting twice a week during that time; and they have scarcely any emolument beside; for the inhabitants of Cassel, who are Calvinists, shew no great passion for dramatic entertainments.

The playhouse is neat, though small. The front gallery, with a convenient room behind, is appropriated to the court. When the Prince or Princess stands up, whether between the acts, or in the time of the representation, all the audience, pit, box, and gallery, immediately arise; and remain in a standing posture till their sovereign sit down.

Since the arrival of these players, the court has been uncommonly brilliant, and the Gala days more frequent. Yesterday was a very splendid one. I then observed in the drawing-room, two persons, neither of whom is a Hessian, saluting each other with great politeness and apparent regard. A little after, one of them touched my shoulder, and, pointing to the other, whispered in my ear,—Prenez garde, Monsieur, de cet homme; c'est un grand coquin.

The other within a few minutes came to me, saying, Croyez vous, Monsieur, que vous puissiez reconnoitre un fou si je vous le montrois?—Le voilà, added he, showing the person who had whispered me before.

I have been since told, by those who know both, that each had hit exactly upon the other's character.

This little trait I have mentioned merely on account of its singularity, and to show you how very different the manners of this court, and the sentiments of the courtiers here with regard to each other, are from those at St. James's.

LETTER LV.

Cassel.

The city of Cassel is situated on the river Fulda. It consists of an old and new town. The former is the largest and most irregular. The new town is well built; and there, as you may believe, the nobility and officers of the court have their houses. The streets are beautiful, but not over-crowded with inhabitants.

Besides the large chateau in the town of Cassel, which is the Landgrave's winter residence, he has several villas and castles in different parts of his dominions. Immediately without the town, there is a very beautiful building, in which he dwells for the most part of the summer The apartments there are neat and commodious, some of them adorned with antique statues of considerable value.

None of the rooms are spacious enough to admit of exercising any considerable number of the troops within their walls; but his Highness sometimes indulges in this favourite recreation on the top of this villa, which has a flat roof, most convenient for that purpose.

Around this are some noble parks and gardens, with a very complete orangery. There is also a menagerie, with a considerable collection of curious animals. I saw there a very fine lioness, which has lately lost her husband— an elephant—three camels in fine condition, one of them milk-white, the other two grey, and much taller than the elephant;—an African deer, a fierce and lively animal, with a skin beautifully spotted;—a very tall rain-deer— several leopards—a bear, and a great variety of monkies.—The collection of birds is still more complete, a great many of which are from the East Indies.

In the academy of arts, which is situated in the new town, are some valuable antiques, and other curiosities, among which is a St. John in Mosaic, done after a picture of Raphaël's, with the following inscription below it:

IMAGINEM S. JOHANNES
EX ITALIA ADVENAM
IN RARUM RARÆ INDUSTRIÆ HUMANÆ MONUMENTUM
HANC COLLOCARI JUSSIT
FREDERICUS II. HASSIÆ LANDGR.
A. M. D. CCLXV.

But this art of copying paintings in Mosaic work, I understand has of late been brought to a much greater degree of perfection at Rome.

In the vestibule is placed the trunk of a laurel tree, with this inscription on the wall behind it.

QUÆ
PER OCTO PRINCIPUM CATTORUM ÆTATIS
IN AMÆNIS INCLYTI CASSEL.
VIRIDARII SPATIAM FLORUIT
LAURUS
ALT. CIRCITER LIV. LAT. IV. PED. RHENAN.
AD TEMPORA HEROUM
SERENISS. DOMUS HASSIÆ
CORONIS CINGENDA,
SENIO, SED NON IMPROLIS, EMORTUA EST
NE VERO TOTA PERIRET
ARBOR APOLLINI SACRA
TRUNCUM IN MUSEO SERVARI JUSSIT
FREDERICUS II. H. L.
A. M. D. CCLXIII.

They also show a sword, which was consecrated by the Pope, and sent to one of the Princes of this family at his setting out on an expedition to the Holy Land. What havoc this sacred weapon made among the infidels I cannot say.—It has a very venerable appearance for a sword, and yet seems little the worse for wear.

Near the old chateau, and a little to one side, is a colonade of small pillars lately built, and intended as an ornament to the ancient castle, though in a very different style of architecture. The slimness of their form appears the more remarkable on account of their vicinity to this Gothic structure.

Some time since, a mountebank came to Cassel, who, besides many other wonderful feats, pretended that he could swallow and digest stones. A Hessian officer walking before the chateau with an English gentleman, who then happened to be at Cassel, asked him, What he thought of the fine new colonade?—It is very fine indeed, replied the stranger; but if you wish it to be durable, you ought to take care not to allow the mountebank to walk this way before breakfast.

Nothing in the country of Hesse is more worthy the admiration of travellers, than the Gothic temple and cascade at Wasenstein. There was originally at this place an old building, which was used by the Princes of this family as a kind of hunting-house. It is situated near the bottom of a high mountain, and has been enlarged and improved at different times. But the present Landgrave's grandfather, who was a Prince of equal taste and magnificence, formed, upon the face of the mountain opposite to this house, a series of artificial cataracts, cascades, and various kinds of water-works, in the noblest style that can be imagined.

The principal cascades are in the middle, and on each side are stairs of large black stones of a flinty texture, brought from a rock at a considerable distance. Each of these stairs consists of eight hundred steps, leading from the bottom to the summit of the mountain; and when the works are allowed to play, the water flowing over them forms two continued chains of smaller cascades. At convenient distances, as you ascend, are four platforms, with a spacious bason in each; also grottos and caves ornamented with shell-work, statues of Naiads, and sea divinities.—One grotto in particular, called the grotto of Neptune and Amphitrite, is happily imagined, and well executed.

The water rushes from the summit of this mountain in various shapes:—Sometimes in detached cascades, sometimes in large sheets like broad crystalline mirrors; at one place, it is broken by a rock consisting of huge stones, artificially placed for that purpose.—There are also fountains, which eject the water in columns of five or six inches diameter to a considerable height.

All this must have a very brilliant effect when viewed from the bottom. This sight, however, I did not enjoy; for there has been a continued frost ever since we have been at Cassel; and when I visited Wasenstein, the fields were covered with snow, which did not prevent my going to the top, though it made the ascent by the flairs exceedingly difficult.

On the highest part of the mountain, a Gothic temple is built, and upon the top of that an obelisk, which is crowned by a colossal statue of Hercules leaning on his club, in the attitude of the Farnese Hercules. This figure is of copper, and thirty feet in height. There is a staircase within the club by which a man may ascend, and have a view of the country from a window at the top.

Wasenstein, upon the whole, is infinitely the noblest work of the kind I ever saw. I have been allured, there is nothing equal to it in Europe. It has not the air of a modern work, but rather conveys the idea of Roman magnificence.

We think of leaving this within a few days for Brunswick.—I shall not close my letter till we get to Gottingen, where we may probably stay a short time.

P. S. The D. and I took our leave of the Court and our friends yesterday, and actually set out from Cassel this morning; but finding the roads entirely overflowed by the extraordinary swelling of the Fulda, we were obliged to return. A great thaw for some days past dissolving the snow and ice, has occasioned this swelling, and rendered the roads impassable.

After taking leave we could not appear again at court, but dined at one of the messes with the officers.—From this party I am just returned, and finding it uncertain when we may get to Gottingen, I send this to-night.

Adieu.

LETTER LVI.

As soon as the roads were passable, we left Cassel, and arrived, not without difficulty and some risk, at Munden, a town situated in a vale, where the Fulda, being joined by another river, takes the name of the Weser.

This town seems to run some danger from inundations. The road, for a considerable way before we entered it, and the streets nearest the river, were still overflowed when we passed.

We went on the same night to Gottingen, an exceedingly neat and well-built town, situated in a beautiful country. The university founded here by George the Second has a considerable reputation. We made but a short stay at Gottingen, and arrived about a month since at Brunswick.

The D—— of H—— had been expected here for some time, and was received by this court with every mark of attention and regard. He was pressed to accept of apartments within the palace, which he thought proper to decline. We sleep every night at private lodgings, but may be said to live at court, as we constantly dine, pass the evening, and sup there, except two days in every week that we dine with the Hereditary Prince and Princess at their apartments.

The family of Brunswick Wolfenbuttle derives not greater lustre from its antiquity, from having given empresses to Germany, and from having a younger branch on the throne of Britain, than from some living characters now belonging to it.

The reigning Duke has that style of conversation, those manners and dispositions, which, in an inferior station of life, would acquire him the character of a sensible, worthy gentleman.

The Duchess is the favourite sister of the King of Prussia. She is fond of study, and particularly addicted to metaphysical inquiries, which, happily, have not shaken, but confirmed her belief in Christianity.

The military fame and public character of Duke Ferdinand are known to all Europe.—In private life, he is of a ceremonious politeness, splendid in his manner of living, attentive even to the minutiæ of his toilet, and fond of variety and magnificence in dress.

He has lived constantly at his brother's court since the D—— of H—— came to Brunswick; but he generally passes the summer in the country.

The Hereditary Prince served under his uncle during the last war, and commanded detached parties of the army with various success. His activity, courage, and thirst of glory, were always conspicuous; but his youthful ardour has been since mellowed by time, study, and reflection; and if he should again appear in the field as a general, it is imagined that he will be as much distinguished for prudence, policy, and judgment, as he ever was for spirit and enterprize. He has at present the rank of Lieutenant-General in the King of Prussia's service, and the command of the garrison at Halberstadt.

I say nothing of his Princess:—Her open cheerful character is well known in England, and her affection for her native country is in no degree diminished by absence.

The Prince Leopold is a very amiable young man. He seems much attached to the D—— of H——, with whom he lives on an intimate and friendly footing.

His sister, the Princess Augusta, is greatly beloved by every body, on account of her obliging temper and excellent disposition.

These illustrious persons always dine and sup together, except two days in the week, as I have already said. With them the officers of the court, and the strangers who are invited, make a company of about twenty or thirty at table.

In the evening the assembly is more numerous. There is a large table for Vingt-un, the Dutchess preferring this game, because a great number of people may be engaged in it together. The reigning Duke and Prince Ferdinand always join in this game.

The Hereditary Princess forms a Quadrille party for herself: Her husband never plays at all. The whole is intended merely for pastime, all kinds of gaming being discouraged. The Dutchess in particular always puts a very moderate stake on her cards.—A man must have very bad luck to lose above twenty pistoles in an evening; so we are in no danger from gaming while at this court.

One wing of the palace is occupied by the Hereditary Prince's family. He has at present three sons and as many daughters, all of the fair complexion, which distinguishes every branch of the Brunswick line.

A few days ago, I accompanied Prince Leopold and the D—— of H—— on a visit to Duke Ferdinand, who was then at his house in the country, about six miles from this place. In that retreat he passes the greatest part of his time. He is fond of gardening, and is now employed in laying out and dressing the ground, in what is called the English taste.

His Serene Highness conducted the D—— round all his park, and shewed him his plans and improvements. The greatest obstacle to the completely beautifying this place, arises from the surface of the country being a dead flat, and incapable of great variety.

The house is surrounded by a Fossé, and contains a great number of apartments. The walls of every room are hung with prints, from the roof to within two feet of the floor. Perhaps there is not so complete a collection of framed ones in any private house or palace in the world. While Prince Ferdinand played at Billiards with the D——— of H———, I continued with Prince Leopold examining these prints, and could scarcely recollect a good one that I did not find here.

His Highness said it was equally difficult and expensive to have a collection of good paintings, and nothing could be more paltry than a bad one: he had therefore taken the resolution to adorn his house with what he certainly could have good of its kind; and next to fine pictures, he thought fine prints the most amusing of all ornaments. But, added he, with a smile, every tolerable room is now perfectly covered, and I have lately received a reinforcement of prints from England, which will oblige me to build new apartments to place them in, puisque je suis toujours accoutumé à donner un poste honorable aux Anglois.

The company had been invited to breakfast; but the repast was a very magnificent dinner, served a little earlier than usual. There was only six persons at table; but the number of attendants might without difficulty have served a company of thirty. The Prince, who is always in the utmost degree polite, was on this occasion remarkably affable and gay. He called toasts after the English custom, and began himself by naming General Conway; he afterwards gave Sir H. Clinton, and continued to toast some British officer as often as it came to his turn.—You may believe it afforded me satisfaction to have had an opportunity of observing a little of the private life of a person who has acted so conspicuous a part on the theatre of Europe.

As he has not returned to the Prussian service, and seems to enjoy rural amusements, and the conversation of a few friends, it is thought he will not again take a part in public affairs, but for the rest of his life repose, in this retreat, on the laurels he gathered in such abundance during the last war.

LETTER LVII.

The town of Brunswick is situated in a plain, on the banks of the Ocker. The houses in general are old, but many new buildings have been erected of late, and the city acquires fresh beauty every day.

Fortifications have been the cause of much calamity to many towns in Germany, having served not to defend them, but rather to attract the vengeance of enemies. For this reason, Cassel, and some other towns, which were formerly fortified, are now dismantled. But the fortifications at Brunswick were of great utility last war, and on one occasion they saved the town from being pillaged, and afforded Prince Frederick, who is now in the Prussian service, an opportunity of performing an action, which, I imagine, gave him more joy than twenty victories. This happened in the year 1761, soon after the battle of Kirch Denkern, when Duke Ferdinand protected Hanover, not by conducting his army into that country, and defending it directly, as the enemy seemed to expert, and probably wished; but by diversion, attacking with strong detachments, commanded by the Hereditary Prince, their magazines in Hesse, and thus drawing their attention from Hanover to that quarter.

While the Duke lay encamped at Willhemsthall, watching the motions of Broglio's army, the Marechal being greatly superior in numbers, sent a body of 20,000 men under Prince Xavier of Saxony, who took possession of Wolfenbuttle, and soon after invested Brunswick.

Prince Ferdinand, anxious to save his native city, ventured to detach 5000 of his army, small as it was, under his nephew, Frederick, assisted by General Luckener, with orders to harass the enemy, and endeavour to raise the siege. The young Prince, while on his march, sent a soldier with a letter to the Governor, which was wrapped round a bullet, and which the soldier was to swallow in case of his being taken by the enemy.—He had the good fortune to get safe into the town.—The letter apprised the commander of the garrison of the Prince's approach, and particularised the night and hour when he expected to be at a certain place near the town, requiring him to favour his entrance.

In the middle of the night appointed, the Prince fell suddenly on the enemy's cavalry, who, unsuspicious of his approach, were encamped carelessly within a mile of the town. They were immediately dispersed, and spread such an alarm among the infantry, that they also retreated with considerable loss.

Early in the morning, the young Prince entered Brunswick, amidst the acclamations of his fellow-citizens, whom he had relieved from the horrors of a siege.—The Hereditary Prince having destroyed the French magazines in Hesse, had been recalled by his uncle, and ordered to attempt the relief of Brunswick. While he was advancing with all possible speed, and had got within a few leagues of the town, he received the news of the siege being raised. On his arrival at his father's palace, he found his brother Frederick at table, entertaining the French officers, who had been taken prisoners the preceding night.

The academy of Brunswick has been new-modelled, and the plan of education improved, by the attention, and under the patronage, of the Hereditary Prince. Students now resort to this academy from many parts of Germany; and there are generally some young gentlemen from Britain, who are sent to be educated here.

Such of them as are intended for a military life, will not find so many advantages united at any other place on the continent, as at the academy of Brunswick. They will here be under the protection of a family partial to the British nation;—every branch of science is taught by matters of known abilities;—the young students will see garrison-duty regularly performed, and may, by the interest of the Prince, obtain liberty to attend the reviews of the Prussian troops at Magdeburg and Berlin:—They will have few temptations to expence, in a town where they can see no examples of extravagance,—have few opportunities of dissipation, and none of gross debauchery.

I passed a day lately at Wolfenbuttle, which is also a fortified city, the ancient residence of this family.—The public library here is reckoned one of the most complete in Germany, and contains many curious manuscripts. They showed us some letters of Luther, and other original pieces in that reformer's own handwriting.

Having dined with Colonel Riedesel, who commands a regiment of cavalry in this town, I returned by Saltzdahlen. This is the only palace I ever saw built almost entirely of wood. There are, nevertheless, some very magnificent apartments in it, and a great gallery of pictures, some of which are allowed by the connoisseurs to be excellent. I will not invade the province of these gentlemen, by presuming to give my opinion of the merits or defects of the pictures, though I have often heard those who are as ignorant as myself, decide upon the interesting subject of painting, in the most dogmatic manner. The terms Contour, Attitude, Casting of Draperies, Charging, Costumé, Passion, Manner, Groupe, Out-line, Chiaro Scuro, Harmony, and Repose, flowed from their tongues, with a volubility that commanded the admiration of all those who could not discover, that in the liberal use of these terms consisted all those gentlemen's taste and knowledge of the fine arts.

Conscious of my ignorance in the mysteries of connoisseurship, I say nothing of the pictures, and presume only to give my opinion, that the gallery which contains them is a very noble room, being two hundred feet long, fifty broad, and forty high.

In this palace there is also a cabinet of china porcelain, containing, as we were told, seven or eight thousand pieces;—and in another smaller cabinet, we were shewn a collection of coarse plates, valuable only on account of their having been painted after designs of Raphaël.

The country about Brunswick is agreeable. I was particularly pleased to see some gentlemen's seats near this town; a sight very rare in Germany, where, if you avoid towns and courts, you may travel over a great extent of country, without perceiving houses for any order of men between the Prince and the Peasant.

I spent yesterday very agreeably fourteen miles from Brunswick, at the house of Mr. de Westphalen. This gentleman attended Duke Ferdinand during the late war in the character of his private secretary; an office which he executed entirely to the satisfaction of that Prince, whose friendship and confidence he still retains.

Mr. de Westphalen has written the history of those memorable campaigns, in which his patron had the command of the allied army, and baffled all the efforts of France in Westphalia. Though this work has been finished long since, the publication has hitherto been delayed for political reasons. It is to appear however at some future period, and is said to be a masterly performance. Indeed, one would naturally suppose this from the remarkable acuteness and sagacity of the author, who was present at the scenes he describes, and knew the secret intentions of the General, whose assistance he has probably had in finishing the work.

LETTER LVIII.

Brunswick.

We have had some masquerade balls here of late.—The Court do not go in procession to these as at Cassel.—Those who chuse to attend, go separately when they find it convenient.

There is a gallery in the masquerade room for the reigning family, where they sometimes sit without masks, and amuse themselves by looking at the dancers. But in general they go masked, and mix in an easy and familiar manner with the company.

I am not surprised that the Germans, especially those of high rank, are fond of masquerades, being so much harassed with ceremony and form, and cramped by the distance which birth throws between people who may have a mutual regard for each other. I imagine they are glad to seize every opportunity of assuming the mask and domino, that they may taste the pleasures of familiar conversation and social mirth.—— In company with the D—— of H——, I once had the honour of dining at the house of a general officer. His sister did the honours of the table; and on the Duke's expressing his surprise that he never had seen her at court, he was told she could not possibly appear there, because she was not noble. This lady, however, was visited at home by the Sovereign, and every family of distinction, all of whom regretted, that the established custom of their country deprived the court of a person whose character they valued so highly.

The General's rank in the army was a sufficient passport for him, but was of no service to his sister; for this etiquette is observed very rigidly with respect to the natives of Germany, though it is greatly relaxed to strangers, particularly the English, who they imagine have less regard for birth and title than any other nation.

Public diversions of every kind are now over for some time, and the Court is at present very thin.—Duke Ferdinand resides in the country. The Hereditary Prince went a few days since to Halberstadt, where he will remain at least a month, to prepare the garrison, and his own regiment in particular, for the grand reviews which are soon to take place. Diligence in duty, and application to the disciplining of the forces, are indispensable in this service. Without these, not all the King's partiality to this Prince, or his consanguinity, could secure to him his uncle's favour for one day, personal talents and vigorous exertion being the sole means of acquiring and retaining the favour of this steady and discerning monarch.

The Hereditary Princess has left Brunswick, and is gone to Zell, and will remain during the absence of her husband with her sister the Queen of Denmark.

The young Prince, Leopold, has also left the Court. He goes directly to Vienna, and it is thought he intends to offer his services to the Emperor. If proper encouragement be given, he will go entirely into the Austrian service. In this case, he will probably, when a war happens, find himself in opposition to his two brothers; a circumstance not much regarded in Germany, where brothers go into different services, with as little hesitation as into different regiments with us.

The strictest friendship has always subsisted between this young man and his sister, who has been crying almost without intermission since he went away.

His mother bears this with more composure, yet her uneasiness is easily perceived. Independent of the absence of her son, she is distressed at the idea of his going into a service, where he may be obliged to act in opposition to her brother, for whom I find she has the greatest affection, as well as the highest admiration.

I was not surprised to hear her speak of him as the greatest man alive; but she extends her eulogium to the qualities of his heart, in which she is not joined by the opinion of all the world.—She, however, dwells particularly on this, calling him the worthiest of men, the firmest friend, and the kindest of brothers:—and as she founds her opinion on her own experience alone, she has the greatest reason to think as she does; for, by every account, the King has always behaved with high regard and undeviating tenderness to her.

The departure of Prince Leopold has revived this Princess's affliction for the untimely fate of two of her sons. One died in the Russian camp at the end of the campaign of 1769, in which he had served with great distinction as a volunteer; the other was killed in a skirmish towards the end of the last war; having received a shot in his throat, he died of the wound fifteen days after, much regretted by the army, who had formed a high idea of the rising merit of this gallant youth.

He wrote a letter to his mother in the morning of the day on which he died. In this letter he regrets, that he should be stopped so soon in the course of honour, and laments that he had not been killed in some memorable action, which would have saved his name from oblivion, or in achieving something worthy of the martial spirit of his family. He expresses satisfaction, however, that his memory would at least be dear to some friends, and that he was certain of living in his mother's affections while she should exist. He then declares his gratitude to her for all her care and tenderness, and concludes with these expressions, which I translate as near as I can remember—I wished the Dutchess to repeat them; but it was with difficulty, and eyes overflowing, that she pronounced them once:—"My eyes grow dim—I can see no longer—happy to have employed their last light in expressing my duty to my mother."

LETTER LIX.

Hanover.

The D—— of H—— having determined to pay his respects to the Queen of Denmark, before he left this country, chose to make his visit while the Hereditary Princess was with her sister.

I accompanied him to Zell, and next day waited on the Count and Countess Dean, to let them know of the D——'s arrival, and to be informed when we could have the honour of being presented to the Queen. They both belong to the Princess of Brunswick's family, and while I was at breakfast with them, her Royal Highness entered the room, and gave me the information I wanted.

Before dinner, I returned with the Duke to the castle, where we remained till late in the evening. There was a concert of music between dinner and supper, and the Queen seemed in better spirits than could have been expected.

Zell is a small town, without trade or manufactures; the houses are old, and of a mean appearance, yet the high courts of appeal for all the territories of the Electoral House of Brunswick Lunenburg are held here; the inhabitants derive their principal means of subsistence from this circumstance.

This town was severely harassed by the French army at the beginning of the late war, and was afterwards pillaged, in revenge for the supposed infraction of the treaty of Closter-Seven. The Duke de Richlieu had his head-quarters here, when Duke Ferdinand re-assembled the troops who had been disarmed, and dispersed, immediately after that convention.

The castle is a stately building, surrounded by a moat, and strongly fortified. It was formerly the residence of the Dukes of Zell, and was repaired lately by order of the King of Great Britain for the reception of his unfortunate sister. The apartments are spacious and convenient, and now handsomely furnished.

The officers of the Court, the Queen's maids of honour, and other attendants, have a very genteel appearance, and retain the most respectful attachment to their ill-fated mistress. The few days we remained at Zell, were spent entirely at Court, where every thing seemed to be arranged in the style of the other small German courts, and nothing wanting to render the Queen's situation as comfortable as circumstances would admit. But by far her greatest consolation is the company and conversation of her sister. Some degree of satisfaction appears in her countenance while the Princess remains at Zell; but the moment she goes away, the Queen, as we were informed, becomes a prey to dejection and despondency. The Princess exerts herself to prevent this, and devotes to her sister all the time she can spare from the duties she owes to her own family. Unlike those who take the first pretext of breaking connections which can no longer be of advantage, this humane Princess has displayed even more attachment to her sister since her misfortunes, than she ever did while the Queen was in the meridian of her prosperity.

The youth, the agreeable countenance, and obliging manners of the Queen, have conciliated the minds of every one in this country. Though she was in perfect health, and appeared cheerful, yet, convinced that her gaiety was assumed, and the effect of a strong effort, I felt an impression of melancholy, which it was not in my power to overcome all the time we remained at Zell.

From Zell we went to Hanover, and on the evening of our arrival, had the pleasure of hearing Handel's Messiah performed. Some of the best company of this place were assembled on the occasion, and we were here made acquainted with old Field-Marshal Sporken, and other people of distinction. Hanover is a neat, thriving and agreeable city. It has more the air of an English town than any other I have seen in Germany, and the English manners and customs gain ground every day among the inhabitants. The genial influence of freedom has extended from England to this place. Tyranny is not felt, and ease and satisfaction appear in the countenances of the citizens.

This town is regularly fortified, and all the works are in exceeding good order. The troops are sober and regular, and perform every essential part of duty well, though the discipline is not so rigid as in some other parts of Germany. Marshal Sporken, who is the head of the army, is a man of humanity; and though the soldiers are severely punished for real crimes, by the sentence of a court martial, he does not permit his officers to order them to be caned for trifles. Caprice is too apt to blend itself with this method of punishing, and men of cruel dispositions are prone to indulge this diabolical propensity, under the pretence of zeal for discipline.

The Hanoverian infantry are not so tall as some of the other German troops, owing to this, that nobody is forced into the service, the soldiers are all volunteers; whereas, in other parts of Germany, the Prince picks the stoutest and tallest of the peasants, and obliges them to become soldiers. It is allowed, that in action no troops can behave better than the Hanoverians; and it is certain, that desertion is not so frequent among them as among other German troops, which can only be accounted for by their not being pressed into the service, and their being more gently used when in it.

It is not the mode here at present, to lay so much stress on the tricks of the exercise as formerly. The officers in general seem to despise many minutiæ, which are thought of the highest importance in some other services. It is incredible to what a ridiculous length this matter is pushed by some.

At a certain parade, where the Sovereign himself was present, and many officers assembled, I once saw a corpulent general-officer start suddenly, as if he had seen something preternatural. He immediately waddled towards the ranks with all the expedition of a terrified gander. I could not conceive what had put his Excellency into a commotion so little suitable to his years and habit of body. While all the spectators were a-tiptoe to observe the issue of this phenomenon, he arrived at the ranks, and in great wrath, which probably had been augmented by the heat acquired in his course, he pulled off one of the soldier's hats, which it seems had not been properly cocked, and adjusted it to his mind. Having regulated the military discipline in this important particular, he returned to the Prince's right-hand, with a strut expressive of the highest self-approbation.

Two days after our arrival here, I walked to Hernhausen, along a magnificent avenue, as broad, and about double the length of the mall at St. James's. The house itself has nothing extraordinary in its appearance; but the gardens are as fine as gardens planned in the Dutch taste, and formed on ground perfectly level, can be. The orangery is reckoned equal to any in Europe. Here is a kind of rural theatre, where plays may be acted during the fine weather. There is a spacious amphitheatre cut out in green seats for the spectators; a stage in the same taste, with rows of trees for side-scenes, and a great number of arbours and summer-rooms, surrounded by lofty hedges, for the actors to retire and dress in.

When the theatre is illuminated, which is always done when masquerades are given, it must have a very fine effect. The groves, arbours, and labyrinths, seem admirably calculated for all the purpose of this amusement.

In these gardens are several large reservoirs and fountains, and on one side, a canal above a quarter of a mile in length. I have not seen the famous jet d'eau, as the water-works have not been played off since I came to Hanover. On the whole, we pass our time very agreeably here. We have dined twice with Baron de Lenth, who has the chief direction of the affairs of this electorate, and at his house have met with the principal inhabitants. I make one of Marshal Sporken's party every night at Whist, and pass most of my time in the society at his house.

The D—— of H—— having promised to meet some company at Brunswick by a certain day, we shall set out for that place to-morrow—but have engaged to pay another visit to Hanover before we go to Berlin.—My next therefore will be from Brunswick, or possibly from this place after our return.

LETTER LX.

We remained a week at Brunswick, and returned to this town about ten days ago. None of the family are there at present, except the Duke and Duchess, and the young Princess, their daughter.

The character of the Sovereign, at every court, has great influence in forming the taste and manners of courtiers. This must operate with increased force in the little courts of Germany, where the parties are brought nearer to each other, and spend the most part of their time together. The pleasure which the Duchess of Brunswick takes in study, has made reading very fashionable among the ladies of that Court: of this her Royal Highness gave me a curious instance the last time I had the honour of seeing her.

A lady, whose education had been neglected in her youth, and who had arrived at a very ripe age without perceiving any inconveniency from the accident, had obtained, by the interest of some of her relations, a place at the Court of Brunswick. She had not been long there, till she perceived that the conversation in the Duchess's apartments frequently turned on subjects of which she was entirely ignorant, and that those ladies had most of her Royal Highness's ear, who were best acquainted with books. She regretted, for the first time, the neglect of her own education; and although she had hitherto considered that kind of knowledge, which is derived from reading, as unbecoming a woman of quality, yet, as it was now fashionable at Court, she resolved to study hard, that she might get to the top of the mode as fast as possible.

She mentioned this resolution to the Duchess, desiring, at the same time, that her Highness would lend her a book to begin. The Duchess applauded her design, and promised to send her one of the usefullest books in her library— it was a French and German dictionary. Some days after, her Highness enquired how she relished the book. Infinitely, replied this studious lady.— It is the most delightful book I ever saw.—The sentences are all short, and easily understood, and the letters charmingly arranged in ranks, like soldiers on the parade; whereas, in some other books which I have seen, they are mingled together in a confused manner, like a mere mob, so that it is no pleasure to look at them, and very difficult to know what they mean. But I am no longer surprised, added she, at the satisfaction your Royal Highness takes in study.

Since our return to Hanover, we have dined twice at the Palace. There is a household established with officers and servants, and the guard is regularly mounted, as at the time when the Electors resided here constantly. The liveries of the pages and servants are the same with those worn by the King's domestic servants at St. James's. Strangers of distinction are entertained at the Palace in a very magnificent manner. The first of the entertainments I saw was given to the D—— of H——, and the other to young Prince George of Hesse Darmstadt, who arrived here a few days since, with Prince Ernest and Prince Charles of Mecklenburg, brothers to the Queen of Great Britain, both of whom are in the Hanoverian service.

Most of my time is spent as formerly, at Marshal Sporken's. The conversation of a man of sense, who has been fifty years in the service, and in high rank during a considerable part of that time, which led him into an intimacy with some of the most celebrated characters of the age, you may be sure is highly interesting. It affords me satisfaction to be informed from such authority, of many transactions in the last war, the common accounts of which are often different, and sometimes contradictory. The Marshal's observations are sensible and candid, and his manner of converting unreserved. He served with the late Marshal Daun in the allied army, opposed to Marshal Saxe, in the war 1741, and has many curious anecdotes illustrating the characters of some of the commanders who conducted the armies during that memorable period. He has a very high opinion of Duke Ferdinand's military character, and declares, that of all the Generals he ever served under, that Prince seemed to him to have the best talents for conducting an army. He says, that as Prince Ferdinand had seldom held councils of war, or communicated to the Generals of his army, any more of his plans than they were to execute, it was difficult for them to form a just opinion of his capacity, while they remained with the army immediately under his command; but that he (Marshal Sporken) had sometimes commanded a detached army, which obliged the Prince to be more communicative, and afforded the Marshal the strongest proofs of the depth of his judgment. Above all things, he admired the perspicuity of his written instructions.—— These, he said, were always accompanied with the most accurate and minute description of the country through which he was to march, every village, rivulet, hollow, wood, or hill on the route, being distinctly particularised, and the most judicious conjectures concerning the enemy's designs added, with directions how to act in various probable emergencies.

Upon the whole, Marshal Sporken seemed convinced that great part of the success of the allies, during the late war in Westphalia, was owing to the foresight, prudence, and sagacity of their General. One memorable event, however, which has been cited as the most striking proof of all these, he imagined was not so much owing to any of them, as to the personal valour of a few regiments, and the good conduct of some inferior officers. The Marshal added, that his praises of Duke Ferdinand's military abilities did not proceed from private attachment, for he could claim no share in his friendship; on the contrary, a misunderstanding had happened between them, on account of an incident at the siege of Cassel, the particulars of which he recapitulated, and this misunderstanding was of a nature never to be made up.

The liberal, candid sentiments of this venerable man carry conviction, and command esteem. He is respected by people of all ranks, and listened to like an oracle. In the society generally to be found at the Marshal's, there are some nearly of his own age, who formed the private parties of George the Second, as often as he came to visit his native country. The memory of that monarch is greatly venerated here. I have heard his contemporaries of this society relate a thousand little anecdotes concerning him, which at once evinced the good disposition of the King, and their own gratitude. From these accounts it appeared, that he was naturally of a very sociable temper, and entirely laid aside, when at Hanover, the state and reserve which he retained in England, living in that familiar and confidential manner which Princes, as well as peasants, will assume in the company of those they love, and who love them.

Not only the personal friends of that monarch speak of him with regard, the same sentiments prevail among all ranks of people in the Electorate. Nothing does more honour to his character, or can be a less equivocal proof of his equity, than his having governed these subjects, over whom he had an unlimited power, with as much justice and moderation as those whose rights are guarded by law, and a jealous constitution.

The two visits I have made to Hanover, have confirmed the favourable impression I had before received of the German character. One of the most disagreeable circumstances which attend travelling is, the being obliged to leave acquaintances after you have discovered their worth, and acquired some degree of their friendship. As the season for the Prussian reviews now approaches, we have already taken leave of our friends, and are to set out to-morrow morning on our return to Brunswick, that after remaining a few days there, we may still get to Potsdam in proper time.

I shall not leave behind me every valuable acquaintance I have acquired since I came to Hanover.—We met, on our last arrival here, with Mr. F———, son of Lord F———. He has been of our parties ever since, and will accompany us to Brunswick and Potsdam.

LETTER LXI.

On returning to Brunswick, we found the Hereditary Princess had come from Zell a few days before, having left the Queen of Denmark in perfect health. The Princess resided with her children at Antonettenruche, a villa a few miles from Brunswick. She invited the D—— of H——, Mr. F——, and me, to dine with her the day before we were to set out for Potsdam. That morning I chanced to take a very early walk in the gardens of the palace.—The Duke of Brunswick was there.—He informed me, that an express had arrived with news of the Queen of Denmark's death.—They had received accounts a few days before that she had been seized with a putrid fever.—He said that nobody in the town or court knew of this, except his own family, and desired that I would not mention it to the Princess, who, he knew, would be greatly affected; for he intended to send a person, after her company should be gone, who would inform her of this event, with all its circumstances.

When we went, we found the Princess in some anxiety about her sister;—yet rather elated with the accounts she had received that day by the post. She showed us her letters.—They contained a general description of the symptoms, and conveyed some hopes of the Queen's recovery. Unable to bear the idea of her sister's death, she wrested every expression into the most favourable sense, and the company met her wishes, by confirming the interpretation she gave. To me, who knew the truth, this scene was affecting and painful.

As we returned to Brunswick in the evening, we met the gentleman who was commissioned by the Duke to impart the news of the Queen's death to her sister.—We supped the same night at court, and took leave of this illustrious family.—The Duchess gave me a letter to her son, Prince Frederick, at Berlin, which she said would secure me a good reception at that capital.

On coming to the inn, we found a very numerous company, and the whole house resounded with music and dancing. It is customary all over Germany, after a marriage of citizens, to give the wedding-feast at an inn. As there was no great chance of our being much refreshed by sleep that night, instead of going to bed, we ordered post-horses, and left Brunswick about three in the morning.

We arrived the same afternoon at Magdeburg. The country all the way is perfectly level. The Duchy of Magdeburg produces fine cattle, and a considerable quantity of corn, those parts which are not marshy, and over-grown with wood, being very fertile. I have seen few or no inclosures in this, or any part of Germany, except such as surround the gardens or parks of Princes.

The King of Prussia has a seat in the diet of the empire, as Duke of Magdeburg. The capital, which bears the same name with the duchy, is a very considerable town, well built and strongly fortified. There are manufactories here of cotton and linen goods, of stockings, gloves, and tobacco; but the principal are those of woollen and silk.

The German woollen cloths are, in general, much inferior to the English and French. The Prussian officers, however, assert, that the dark blue cloth made here, and in other parts of the King of Prussia's dominions, though coarser, wears better, and has a more decent appearance when long worn, than the finest cloth manufactured in England or France.—Thus much is certain, that the Prussian blue is preferable to any other cloth made in Germany.—The town of Magdeburg is happily situated for trade, having an easy communication with Hamburg by the Elbe, and lying on the road between Upper and Lower Germany. It is also the strongest place belonging to his Prussian Majesty, and where his principal magazines and foundries are established. In time of war, it is the repository of whatever he finds necessary to place out of the reach of sudden insult.

Places where any extraordinary event has happened, even though they should have nothing else to distinguish them, interest me more than the most flourishing country, or finest town which has never been the scene of any thing memorable. Fancy, awakened by the view of the former, instantly gives shape and features to men we have never seen.—We hear them speak, and see them act; the passions are excited, the mind amused; the houses, the rivers, the fields around supplying the absence of the poet and historian, and restoring with new energy the whole scene to the mind.

While crossing the Elbe at this town with the D—— of H——, I recalled to his memory the dreadful tragedy which was acted here by the Austrian General Tilly, who having taken this town by storm, delivered up the citizens, without distinction of age or sex, to the barbarity and lust of his soldiers. Besides the general massacre, they exhibited such acts of wanton cruelty, as disgrace human nature. We viewed with a lively sympathy, that part of the river where three or four hundred of the inhabitants got over and made their escape:—all that were saved out of twenty thousand citizens!

This sad catastrophe supplied us with conversation for great part of this day's journey. It is unnecessary to comment on an event of this kind to a person of the D——'s sensibility.—Proper reflections arise spontaneously in a well-formed mind from the simple narrative.

The country is well cultivated, and fertile for about two leagues beyond Magdeburg; afterwards it becomes more barren, and within a few leagues of Brandenburg, it is as naked and sandy as the deserts of Arabia.

Brandenburg, from which the whole Electorate takes its name, is but a small town, divided into Old and New by a river, which separates the fort from both. The principal trade is carried on by some French woollen manufacturers, whom the King has encouraged to reside at this town. The whole number of inhabitants does not amount to more than 1500.

On entering the Prussian garrison towns, you are stopped at the gate; the officer of the guard asks your name, whence you come, whither you are going, and takes your answers down in writing. This is done in the French garrisons also, but not with the same degree of form and accuracy.

When the title of Duke is given, the guard generally turns out under arms. As for Milord, it is a title treated with very little ceremony, either in France or Germany. It is often assumed in foreign countries by those who have no right to it, and given to every Englishman of a decent appearance. But Duke, in Germany, implies a Sovereign, and is more respectable than Prince. Every son of a Duke in this country, is called Prince, although he had as many as old King Priam.

We arrived last night at Potsdam, which important piece of news, you will please to observe, I have taken the earliest opportunity of communicating.

LETTER LXII.

Potsdam.

The day after our arrival here, I waited on the Count Finkenstein, and desired to know when the D—— of H—— and I could have the honour of being presented to the King, requesting, at the same time, the liberty of attending at the reviews. I was not a little surprised when this minister told me, that I must write a letter to his Majesty, informing him of that request, and that I should certainly receive an answer the day following. It appeared very singular to write to so great a Prince upon an affair of such small importance; but the Count told me this was the established rule. So I immediately did as I was desired.

Next morning one of the court-servants called for me at the inn, and delivered a sealed letter addressed to me, and signed by the King, importing, that as the court would soon be at Berlin, the minister in waiting there would let the D—— of H—— and Mr. —— know when they might be presented, and that they were very welcome to attend at all the reviews.

In the evening we were presented to the Prince and Princess of Prussia, who reside almost constantly at Potsdam. He is a tall, stout-made, handsome man, of about thirty-five years of age. The Princess is of the family of Hesse-Darmstadt, and has a great resemblance to her aunt, whom we had seen at Carlsruhe. We have had the honour of supping with them twice during the few days we have been at Potsdam.

The Prince and all the officers have been employed every morning in preparing for the reviews. Yesterday, for the second time, there were seven thousand men reviewed by the King. The Prince of Prussia's son, a child of six or seven years old, was present on foot with his tutor, and unattended by any officer or servant. They mingled without any mark of distinction among the other spectators. I mentioned my surprise at this to the tutor. In France, said he, it would be otherwise: the Dauphin, at the age of this child, would be carried to the review in a coach, with a troop of musqueteers to attend him; but here, the King and Prince are equally desirous that their successor should be brought up in a hardy manner, and without any strong impression of his own importance. Sentiments of that kind will come soon enough, in spite of all the pains that can be taken to exclude them.

The troops were drawn up in one line along the summits of some hills. From this situation they descended over very unequal and rough ground, firing in grand divisions all the way, till they came to the plain, where they went through various evolutions. But as we were to set out in a little time for Berlin, where the grand reviews of that garrison are to take place, I shall say no more on the subject of reviews till then.

Our mornings, since we came hither, have always been passed with the troops in the field. The forenoons we have spent in looking at every thing curious in the town. The houses are built of a fine white free-stone, almost all of them new, and nearly of the same height. The streets are regular and well paved, and there are some very magnificent public buildings; so that Potsdam has every requisite to form an agreeable town, if by that word is meant the streets, stone-walls, and external appearance. But if a more complex idea be annexed to the word, and if it be thought to comprehend the finishing, furniture, and conveniencies within the houses, in that case Potsdam is a very poor town indeed.

The King having expressed a great inclination to see this town increase, several monied people built houses, partly to pay their court to his Majesty, and partly because, by letting them, they found they would receive very good interest for their money. But as the town did not augment so quickly as he wished, his Majesty ordered several streets to be built at once, at his own expence. This immediately sunk the value of houses, and the first builders found they had disposed of their money very injudiciously.

Towns generally are formed by degrees, as the inhabitants increase in numbers; and houses are built larger and more commodious as they increase in riches; for men's ideas of conveniency enlarge with their wealth. But here the matter is reversed: the houses are reared in the first place, in hopes that their fair outsides, like the nymphs of Circe, will allure travellers, and attract inhabitants. Hitherto their power of attraction has not been strong; for few towns are worse inhabited than Potsdam, though the houses are let to merchants and trades-people at very small rents.

I was not a little surprised, while I walked through the town, to see buff-belts, breeches and waistcoats, hanging to dry from the genteelest looking houses, till I was informed, that each housekeeper has two or more soldiers quartered in his house, and their apartments are, for the most part, on the first floor, with windows to the street; which I am told is also the case at Berlin. The King chooses that his soldiers should be quartered with the citizens, rather than in barracks. This ought to be a sufficient answer to those military gentlemen, who insist on building barracks for the soldiers in Britain, upon the supposition, that our army cannot be well disciplined without them.

For it could scarcely be expected, or wished, that the British army were under more rigid discipline than the Prussian.

I imagine the Prussian soldiers are quartered in private houses rather than barracks, from considerations diametrically opposite to those which produce the same effect in England.—The British parliament have always shown an aversion to lodging the military in barracks, and have preferred quartering them in the citizens' houses, that a connection and good-will may be cultivated between the soldiers and their fellow-citizens; and that the former may not consider themselves as a distinct body of men, with a separate interest from the rest of the community, and whose duty it is implicitly to obey the will of the crown at all times, and upon all occasions.

Whereas here it may not be thought expedient, to lodge great bodies of armed men together in barracks, lest they should, during the night, form combinations destructive of discipline, and dangerous to government. This cannot happen in the day-time, because then the officers are present, and the soldiers are not allowed even to speak to each other when under arms; and while off duty, their time is wholly filled up in cleaning their arms, accoutrements, and clothes, and preparing for the next guard.—I imagine these may be part, at least, of the reasons which induce the King of Prussia to prefer quartering his men in private houses; for in all other respects, lodging them together in barracks would be more convenient, and more agreeable to the genius of his government.

The palace at Potsdam, or what they call the castle, is a very noble building, with magnificent gardens adjacent. I shall not trouble you with a description of either, only it struck me as a thing rather uncommon in a palace, to find the study by far the finest apartment in it. The ornaments of this are of massy silver. The writing-desk, the embellishments of the table, and the accommodations for the books, were all in fine taste.

The person who attended us, asked if we had any desire to see his Majesty's wardrobe?—On being answered in the affirmative, he conducted us to the chamber where the monarch's clothes are deposited; it had a very different appearance from his library. The whole wardrobe consisted of two blue coats, faced with red, the lining of one a little torn;—two yellow waistcoats, a good deal soiled with Spanish snuff;—three pair of yellow breeches, and a suit of blue velvet, embroidered with silver, for grand occasions.

I imagined at first, that the man had got a few of the King's old clothes, and kept them here to amuse strangers; but, upon enquiry, I was assured, that what I have mentioned, with two suits of uniform which he has at Sans-Souci, form the entire wardrobe of the King of Prussia. Our attendant said, he had never known it more complete. As for the velvet suit, it was about ten years of age, and still enjoyed all the vigour of youth. Indeed, if the moths spared it as much as his Majesty has done, it may last the age of Methusalem.—In the same room, are some standards belonging to the cavalry. Instead of the usual square flag, two or three of these have the figures of eagles in carved silver fixed on a pole.

In the bed-chamber where the late King died, at the lower part of the window which looks into the garden, four panes have been removed, and a piece of glass equal in size to all the four supplies their place. We were informed that his late Majesty's supreme delight through life had been to see his troops exercise, and that he had retained this passion till his last breath. When he was confined to his room by his last illness, he used to sit and view them through the window, which had been framed in this manner, that he might enjoy these dying contemplations with the greater conveniency. Becoming gradually weaker by the increasing distemper, he could not sit, but was obliged to lie on a couch through the day. When at any time he was uncommonly languid, they raised his head to the window, and a sight of the men under arms was perceived to operate like a cordial, and revive his spirits.—By frequent repetition, however, even this cordial lost its effect.— His eyes became dim—when his head was raised, he could no longer perceive the soldiers, and he expired.

This was feeling the ruling passion as strong in death as any man ever felt it.

LETTER LXIII.

I have been twice or thrice at Sans-Souci, which is at a small distance from Potsdam. The King lives constantly at the Old Palace, except when some people of very great distinction come to reside with him for some days. He then receives them at the New Palace, and remains there himself during their stay.

The gallery contains a great collection of paintings, some of them originals, highly esteemed.—The most valuable are of the Flemish school.—Some people who pass for connoisseurs, and for aught I know may be what they pretend, assert, that the King has not a just taste in painting, which appears by his purchasing a great many very indifferent pictures. Whatever may be in that, it is certain that his Majesty does not give the least importance to the opinion of these connoisseurs; but buys, admires, and avows his admiration of such pieces as appear excellent in his own eyes, without regarding what they or others may think. It has no weight with him, that the piece is said to be by Raphaël, Guido, or Corregio. If he see no beauty in it, he says so, and without ceremony prefers the work of a modern or obscure painter.

This is considered by many critics in painting as blasphemy, and shocks them more than any other species of impiety. A painter and great connoisseur whom the King had disgusted, by rejecting some pictures of his recommending, and by purchasing others which he had condemned, said (speaking of the King), The man imagines, because he can play on the German flute, and has been praised by a parcel of poets and philosophers, and has gained ten or a dozen battles, that therefore he understands painting; but fighting battles is one thing, and a true knowledge of painting is another, and that he will find to his cost.

A few years after the late war, the King of Prussia began to build the new palace of Sans-Souci, which is now completely finished, and is certainly a very noble and splendid work. The offices are at a considerable distance, and are joined to the body of the palace by a double colonnade, which has a very grand effect. The front of the palace seems rather crowded, by the great number of statues which are intended to ornament it. These are generally in groups, representing some story from Ovid. This building has a cupola, terminated by a large crown, supported by the three Graces. The D——— of H——— observed, that three Prussian grenadiers would have been more suitable. On the ground-floor, in the middle, there is a large hall, whose floor, sides, and roof, are all of marble. It is called the grotto, and the ornaments correspond with that name. This room can be agreeable only when the weather is excessively hot. In Italy it would be delightful. The roof of this hall is low, and vaulted, and supports another room in all respects of the same dimensions, only higher. This second room is also lined with beautiful marble. The other apartments are adorned with rich furniture and paintings, all very showy. Many people think them gaudy.—It must be owned, that the gilding is laid on with a very lavish hand.

Opposite to the old palace of Sans-Souci, and immediately without the gardens, Lord Marechal has built a house, where he constantly resides. You are well acquainted with the amiable character of this nobleman. We waited on him soon after our arrival, and have dined with him several times since. On the front of his house is this inscription:

FREDERICUS II. NOBIS HÆC OTIA FECIT.

Adjoining to this house is a small garden, with a door which communicates with the King's garden of Sans-Souci, so that his Lordship has the full enjoyment of these gardens. The King has also a key to my Lord's little garden, and frequently walks by this passage to visit him.

We set out for Berlin to-morrow. Adieu.

LETTER LXIV.

Berlin.

We arrived here in the height of the preparation for the reviews. Nothing was to be seen in the streets but soldiers parading, and officers hurrying backwards and forwards. The town looked more like the cantonment of a great army, than the capital of a kingdom in the time of profound peace. The Court itself resembled the levee of a General in the field—except the foreign ministers, and a few strangers, every man there (for there were no women) was dressed in a military uniform.

Mr. Harris, the British minister, attended the D—— of H——, the day we were presented to the King. A son of Prince Kaunitz's, and some other strangers, were presented at the same time. The Count Reuse, chamberlain of the Court, named each person to his Majesty as he approached. He conversed a considerable time with the D——, and spoke a few words to every person who was presented.—His countenance and manner are exceedingly animated.—He seemed that day in very high spirits, and spoke to all his officers in an easy style, and with a kind of gay affability. On their part, they appear before their master with an erect military boldness, free from that cringing address which prevails in many Courts, but would not succeed here.

The King was three days at Berlin before the reviews began, and passed some hours every morning in the park, where there were four or five thousand men ordered daily, not to be exercised, but simply that the King might examine the state of each corps in particular: and it is incredible with what accuracy and minute attention he did examine them, the Colonel of the regiment under scrutiny walking along with him, to answer any question, and hear his directions and remarks. By this exactness, he not only knows the condition of the army in general, but the appearance, degree of discipline, and strength of each regiment.

The whole number reviewed was about thirty-six or thirty-eight thousand, consisting of the garrison of Berlin, and troops from some of the adjacent towns and villages. This army was in the field three mornings successively, and the operations were different each day. I shall endeavour to give you an idea of the plan of the last day's review, which is freshest in my memory.

At break of day, about eight thousand men marched out of Berlin, under the command of a general officer, and took possession of a village, situated on a rising ground, at the distance of two or three miles. About an hour after, the King himself joined the army, which was assembled without the gates. He divided it into three columns. Two general officers took the command of two of them; he himself led the third. The whole marched by three different routes towards the village, where the former detachment had now taken post. In the attack and defence of this village the review consisted.

As the army advanced, they were cannonaded from the village, but could not be supposed to suffer much, because the leader of each column advanced with caution, taking such circuits as exposed the men very little.

At length the three columns met on a large plain near the village, but protected from the batteries by a rising of the ground. Here the King formed the army into two lines. While this was doing, they were perfectly secure; but they could not advance towards the village otherwise than by going over the swell in the ground, and being exposed to all the cannon of the enemy. This was to be performed, therefore, with as much expedition as could be consistent with good order. The right wing of the army made the attack. As soon as the signal was given, all the drums and fifes struck up at once. The soldiers advanced with a rapid pace. A numerous train of large field-pieces, placed at proper intervals, advanced with equal velocity, and kept in a line with the front rank. The rapidity with which they were charged and discharged as they advanced was quite astonishing. When the line came within a proper distance of the village, the soldiers began to use their firelocks. In the mean time there was a furious cannonade, and discharge of small shot from the village. The King was between the advancing line and the village during the attack. When they had got very near the hedges, a new battery opened from the village. The King gave a signal, and the first line broke, fell into an artificial confusion, and gave back towards the second line, which opened at several places, and closed again the moment the retreating line had pierced through. The second line then moved to the attack, as the former had done. This also seemed to be repulsed—a retreat was sounded, and the whole wing began to retire. A body of cavalry then appeared from the village, and were advancing to charge the retreating army, but were themselves charged, and driven back, by the cavalry of the right wing.

A body of hussars pursued also from the village, and harassed the retreating army. These were sometimes repulsed by the soldiers, who turned and fired on them, and sometimes by detached parties of cavalry, which drove them away.

These various operations lasted from five in the morning till noon, when the troops returned to Berlin.—It is hardly possible for any words of mine to convey an adequate idea of the perfect manner in which these evolutions were executed. The charges made by the cavalry were praised by the King himself. I had never seen so great a body together, and had no idea that it was possible to charge at full gallop, and keep the ranks and distances so exactly as they did.

Upon the principle, that velocity is equal to weight, they endeavour to compensate for the lightness of the horses by the quickness of their motion. The hussars in the Prussian army are taught, not only to harass a retreating army in detached parties, but to charge like heavy cavalry in a large body. The late General Seidlitz, who had the reputation of being the best officer of cavalry in Europe, brought the Prussian dragoons to a wonderful degree of perfection, and it is said that he gained the battle of Rosbach by one brisk charge. Ever since, the King of Prussia has bestowed great attention on his cavalry. They are now habituated to charge in large bodies, and at full speed.

The cuirassiers are the flower of the Prussian army. They are dressed in buff coats, and wear very heavy iron breastplates, which cover all the fore-part of the body, and have been tried by musket-shot before they are delivered to the men.

I neglected to mention, that the infantry were ordered to shout as they advanced to the attack on the village, and that this practice is adopted by the Prussians in actual service. The King, as I am informed, is of opinion, that this keeps up the spirits of the men, and prevents them from reflecting on the danger of their situation. There are a greater proportion of drummers in the Prussian service than in most others: a regulation, in all probability, founded on the same principle.

The evening after the reviews, there were a concert and supper at Prince Henry's palace. The Queen was present, and the King's brothers, Henry himself, and Ferdinand, with their Princesses; also the Prince and Princess of Prussia, Prince Frederick of Brunswick and his Princess, and a numerous company. I here delivered to Prince Frederick the letter I had brought from his mother, who I found had before apprized him of my intention to go to Berlin.

The King himself was not present. He seldom appears at festivals. All his hours, not employed in business, he spends in reading, or in the society of a few people whom he esteems. The Hereditary Prince of Brunswick is at present the King's most constant companion, a choice which does not more honour to the Prince than to the King's discernment.

Prince Henry's palace is one of the most magnificent buildings in Berlin. No subject of the King of Prussia lives in a more sumptuous manner than this Prince, who keeps a numerous establishment of servants, mostly handsome young men, very richly dressed. The entertainment on this occasion was remarkably splendid.

LETTER LXV.

Berlin.

The day after the reviews, the King, attended by his nephew, the Prince of Prussia, and the Hereditary Prince of Brunswick, set out for Magdeburg, where there is a camp of 15,000 men. He afterwards will proceed to Silesia, and his new acquired dominions in Poland, and is not expected at Potsdam for six weeks at least.

His Majesty makes the same circuit twice every year.—Surely no King in Europe can have such a thorough knowledge of his dominions and subjects as this monarch.—His absence from Berlin has made but little relaxation in the duty, and none in the discipline of the troops. The reviews were scarcely over, when field-days began. There are 1500 or 2000 of the troops belonging to this garrison, exercised in the park almost every morning, besides those who appear on the parade for the ordinary guards.

A review, such as that which I endeavoured to describe, is undoubtedly one of the finest shows that can be exhibited: but when a spectator of sensibility reflects on the means by which these poor fellows are brought to this wonderful degree of accuracy, he will pay a severe tax for this splendid exhibition.—The Prussian discipline on a general view is beautiful; in detail it is shocking.

When the young rustic is brought to the regiment, he is at first treated with a degree of gentleness; he is instructed by words only how to walk, and to hold up his head, and to carry his firelock, and he is not punished, though he should not succeed in his earliest attempts:—they allow his natural aukwardness and timidity to wear off by degrees:—they seem cautious of confounding him at the beginning, or driving him to despair, and take care not to pour all the terrors of their discipline upon his astonished senses at once. When he has been a little familiarised to his new state, he is taught the exercise of the firelock, first alone, and afterwards with two or three of his companions. This is not entrusted to a corporal or serjeant; it is the duty of a subaltern officer. In the park at Berlin, every morning may be seen the Lieutenants of the different regiments exercising with the greatest assiduity, sometimes a single man, at other times three or four together; and now, if the young recruit shows neglect or remissness, his attention is roused by the officer's cane, which is applied with augmenting energy, till he has acquired the full command of his firelock.—He is taught steadiness under arms, and the immobility of a statue;—he is informed, that all his members are to move only at the word of command, and not at his own pleasure;—that speaking, coughing, sneezing, are all unpardonable crimes; and when the poor lad is accomplished to their mind, they give him to understand, that now it is perfectly known what he can do, and therefore the smallest deficiency will be punished with rigour. And although he should destine every moment of his time, and all his attention, to cleaning his arms, taking care of his clothes, and practising the manual exercise, it is but barely possible for him to escape punishment; and if his captain happens to be of a capricious or cruel disposition, the ill-fated soldier loses the poor chance of that possibility.

As for the officers, they are not indeed subjected to corporal punishment, but they are obliged to bestow as unremitting attention on duty as the men. The subalterns are almost constantly on guard, or exercising the recruits: the Captain knows, that he will be blamed by his Colonel, and can expect no promotion, if his company be not as perfect as the others: the Colonel entirely loses the King's favour if his regiment should fail in any particular: the General is answerable for the discipline of the brigade, or garrison, under his immediate command. The King will not be satisfied with the General's report on that subject, but must examine every thing himself; so that from his Majesty, down to the common centinel, every individual is alert. And as the King, who is the chief spring and primum mobile of the whole, never relaxes, the faculties of every subordinate person are kept in constant exertion: the consequence of which is, that the Prussian army is the best disciplined, and the readiest for service at a minute's warning, of any now in the world, or perhaps that ever was in it. Other monarchs have attempted to carry discipline to the same degree of perfection, and have begun this plan with astonishing eagerness. But a little time and new objects have blunted their keenness, and divided their attention. They have then delegated the execution to a commander in chief, he to another of inferior rank, and thus a certain degree of relaxation having once taken place, soon pervades the whole system; but the perseverance of the King of Prussia is without example, and is perhaps the most remarkable part of his extraordinary character.

That degree of exertion which a man of a vigorous mind is capable of making on some very important occasion, the King of Prussia has made for thirty years at a stretch, without permitting pleasure, indolence, disgust, or disappointment, to interrupt his plan for a single day.—And he has obliged every person through the various departments of his government to make, as far as their characters and strength could go, the same exertions.—I leave you to judge in what manner such a man must be served, and what he is capable of performing.

LETTER LXVI.

Berlin.

No condition in life can be more active, and at the same time have less variety in it, than that of a Prussian officer in the time of peace. He is continually employed in the same occupation, and continually occupied in the same place. There is no rotation of the troops as in the British service. The regiments which were placed in Berlin, Magdeburg, Schweidnitz, and the other garrisons at the conclusion of the war, remain there still. It is dreaded, that if they were occasionally moved from one garrison to another, the foreigners in the service, who are exceedingly prone to desertion, might then find opportunities, which according to the present plan they cannot: for however desirous a Prussian soldier may be to desert, the thing is almost impossible. The moment a man is missing, a certain number of cannons are fired, which announce the desertion to the whole country. The peasants have a considerable reward for seizing a deserter, and are liable to severe penalties if they harbour, or aid him in making his escape, and parties from the garrisons are sent after him in every direction.

As none of the soldiers are ever allowed to go without the walls of the town, it requires great address to get over this first difficulty; and when they have been so far fortunate, many chances remain against their escaping through the Prussian dominions; and even when they arrive safe in any of the neighbouring states,

Nunc eadem fortuna viros tot casibus actos

Insequitur.

For there they will probably be obliged to inlist again as soldiers; so that on the whole, however unhappy they may be, it is absurd to attempt desertion in any other way than by killing themselves, which method, as I am told, begins to prevail.

In consequence of their remaining constantly in the same place, conversing always with the same people, and being employed uniformly in the same business, the Prussian officers acquire a staid, serious appearance, exceedingly different from the gay, dissipated, degagé air of British or French officers. Their only amusement, or relaxation from the duties of their profession, seems to be walking on the parade, and conversing with each other. The inferior officers, thus deprived of opportunities of mixing in general society, and not having time for study, can have no very extensive range of ideas. Their knowledge, it must be confessed, is pretty much confined to that branch of tactics in which they are so much employed; and many of them at length seem to think, that to stand firm and steady, to march erect, to wheel to the right and left, and to charge and discharge a firelock, if not the sole use of human creatures, is at least the chief end of their creation.

The King, as I have been informed, has no inclination that they should reason on a larger compass of thought, which might possibly lead them to despise their daily employment of drilling soldiers, counting the buttons of their coats, and examining the state of their spatter-dashes and breeches. For as soon as men's minds become superior to their business, the business will not be so well performed. Some application to other studies, and opportunities of mixing with a more general society, might make them more agreeable men, but not better captains, lieutenants, and adjutants.

His Majesty imagines he will always find a sufficient number of men of a more liberal turn of mind, and more extensive notions, for officers of great trust and separate commands, where the general must act according to emergencies, and the light of his own understanding. He believes also, that this general system will not deprive him of the advantage of particular exceptions, or prevent genius from being distinguished, when it exists in the humblest spheres of his service. As often, therefore, as he observes any dawnings of this kind; when any officer, or even soldier, discovers uncommon talents, or an extensive capacity, he is sure to be advanced, and placed in a situation where his abilities may have a full power of exertion; while those must stand still, or be moved by a very slow gradation, who have no other merit to depend on for promotion but assiduity alone, which, in the Prussian service, can never conduct to that rank in the army, where other qualifications are wanted.

As to the common men, the leading idea of the Prussian discipline is to reduce them, in many respects, to the nature of machines; that they may have no volition of their own, but be actuated solely by that of their officers; that they may have such a superlative dread of those officers as annihilates all fear of the enemy; and that they may move forwards when ordered, without deeper reasoning or more concern than the firelocks they carry along with them.

Considering the length to which this system is carried, it were to be wished that it could be carried still further, and that those unhappy men, while they retained the faculties of hearing and obeying orders, could be deprived of every other kind of feeling.

The common state of slavery in Asia, or that to which people of civil professions in the most despotic countries are subject, is freedom in comparison of this kind of military slavery. The former are not continually under the eyes of their tyrants, but for long intervals of time may enjoy life without restraint, and as their taste dictates; but all the foreign soldiers in this service, and those of the natives, who are suspected of any intention to desert, and consequently never allowed furloughs, are always under the eye of somebody, who has the power, and too often the inclination, to controul every action of their bodies, and every desire of their hearts.

Since such a number of men all over Europe are doomed to this state of constraint, it is much to be lamented that, from the nature of the service, the doom should fall on the useful, industrious peasantry, who, when uncontrolled by cruel and absurd policy, pass their days in cheerfulness, tasting every real pleasure without the nausea of satiety, or the stings of remorse, and perhaps, of all mankind, have the greatest enjoyment of life. The sum-total of happiness, destroyed by removing men from this situation into a state of misery, must be infinitely greater than if many of the useless, wealthy, and luxurious could be translated into the same state. This would not be annihilating happiness, but only shifting the scene of the wretched. Such recruits would only be harassed by the caprices of others instead of their own;—plagued with the manual exercise, instead of being tortured by peevishness and disgust;—laid up in consequence of running the gantlet, instead of being laid up with the gout;—and, finally, knocked down by a cannon-ball, instead of being killed by a fit of the apoplexy or a surfeit.

LETTER LXVII.

Berlin.

Instead of troubling you with any more observations of my own, on the nature of the Prussian discipline, or the principles on which it is founded, I shall give you the substance of some conversations I have had on that subject with a Prussian officer of character.

Walking one morning in the park, we saw a poor fellow smartly caned, for no other reason, but because he did not return the ram-rod into his piece with so much celerity as the rest of the platoon. I turned away with indignation from the sight, which the officer observing, said, You think the punishment too severe for the crime?—There was no crime, said I: the ram-rod slipt through his fingers by accident, and it is not possible to imagine, that the man had any intention to perform this important motion less rapidly than his comrades. Every thing must be considered as of importance by a soldier, replied my Prussian acquaintance, which his officer orders him to do. In all probability, the fault was involuntary; but it is not always possible to distinguish involuntary faults from those that happen through negligence. To prevent any man from hoping that his negligence will be forgiven as involuntary, all blunders are punished, from whatever cause they happen; the consequence of which is, that every man is more attentive and alert than he would otherwise be. I remember, added he, that it was very usual on field-days for the dragoons to have their hats blown off. Nobody suspected that they had bribed the wind to play this trick; yet a general officer being put out of humour by the frequency of the accident, gave orders to punish every man to whom it should happen; and since that order was put in force, the hats have been much seldomer blown off.

I then mentioned a fact which appeared to me still more extraordinary. A hussar, at the last review, had fallen from his horse at full gallop, and was so much bruised, that it was found necessary to carry him to the hospital; and I had been assured, that as soon as the man should be perfectly recovered, he would certainly be punished for having fallen. Now, continued I, though a man may be a little careless about his hat, it cannot be imagined, that this hussar was not seriously inclined to keep his seat; for by falling, he might have broke his neck, or have been trod to death: Or, even if you choose to suppose, that he did not ride with all the attention he ought, yet, as he received one severe punishment by the fall, it would be cruel to inflict another. I have nothing to oppose to the solidity of your argument, replied the Prussian, but that General Seidlitz, who was the best officer of cavalry in the world, first introduced this piece of cruelty, since which it is certain, that the men have not fallen so often. The King imagines, continued the Prussian, that discipline is the soul of an army; that men in the different nations of Europe are, in those qualities which are thought necessary for a soldier, nearly on a par; that in two armies of equal numbers, the degrees of discipline will determine how far one is superior to the other. His great object, therefore, is to keep his own army at the highest possible degree of perfection in this essential point. If that could be done by gentle means, undoubtedly he would prefer them.—He is not naturally of a cruel disposition.—His general conduct to officers of rank proves this.—Finding that the hopes of promotion, and a sense of honour, are sufficient motives to prompt them to their duty, he never has had recourse, except in cases of treachery, to any higher punishment than dismissing them. In some remarkable instances, he has displayed more mildness than is usual in any other service. Some of his Generals have allowed towns of the greatest importance to be taken by surprise; others have lost intire armies; yet he never was influenced by popular clamour, or by the ruinous condition of his own affairs in consequence of those losses, to put any of the unfortunate generals to death. And when any of them have been suspended for a certain time, or declared, by the decree of a court-martial, incapable of a military command under him, he has never aggravated the sentence by any opprobrious commentary, but has rather alleviated it by some clause or message, which spared the honour of the condemned general.

The common soldiers cannot be kept to their duty by mild treatment. Severe and immediate corporal punishment is found absolutely necessary.—Not to use it at all, or to use it in a degree incapable of producing the full effect, would be weakness. Soldiers are sometimes punished for slips, which perhaps all their attention cannot prevent; because, though it is impossible to ascertain, that any particular man could have avoided them, yet experience has taught, that, by punishing every blunder, fewer are committed on the whole. This sufficiently justifies the practice of what you call cruelty, but which is in reality salutary discipline; for an individual suffering unjustly is not so great an evil in an army, as the permitting negligence to pass unpunished. To allow ten guilty men to escape, rather than risk the punishment of one innocent person, may be a good maxim in morality, or in civil government, but the reverse will be found preferable in military discipline.

When the Prussian had finished his discourse, I said, You seem to neglect all those incitements which are supposed to influence the minds of soldiers; the love of glory, the love of country, you count as nothing. You address yourself to no passion but one.—Fear is the only instrument by which you compel your common men to deeds of intrepidity.—Never mind the instrument, replied the Prussian, but look to the effect.

I am convinced, answered I, that British soldiers, with that degree of discipline which subsists in our army, which is not near so rigid as yours, animated by their native courage, and the interest which even the common men take in all their country's quarrels, are at least equal to any other troops.

I hope, said he, the experiment will not be made soon, for I esteem your nation, and should be sorry to see your troops opposed to ours in the field: but till they are, you cannot be sure of the justness of your assertion. The advantages you gained over the French in the late war rather makes for my argument, because the French army is more remiss in the article of discipline than yours.

I then returned to my old ground, the cruelty of harassing and tormenting men without intermission; and asserted, that the advantages arising from such excessive severity, even though they should be as great as he represented, could not form a sufficient reason for rendering the lives of so many men miserable.

I do not know that they are miserable, replied he—When men are but indifferently fed, forced to perform very hard duty, certain of being severely punished for the smallest faults, and sometimes even for their misfortunes, can you doubt, said I, that these men are miserable?—They do not seem miserable, replied he, they bear it very well.—— And would you, added I, have the less remorse in tormenting men, because they have the strength of mind to bear it well?

I then told him a story I had heard of an English sailor, who was tried for a robbery he had committed on the highway. While his doom was pronouncing, he raised a piece of rolled tobacco to his mouth, and held it between his teeth till he heard the sentence of death passed on him. He then bit off a piece of the tobacco, and began to chew it with great unconcern. Sirrah, said the judge, piqued at the man's indifference, do you know that you are to be hanged in a very short time?—So I hear, said the sailor, squirting a little tobacco juice from his mouth.—Do you know, rejoined the judge, where you will go when you die?—I cannot tell indeed, an't please your honour, said the sailor.—Why, then, cried the judge, with a tremendous voice, I will tell you: You will go to hell, you villain, and there be burnt to all eternity.—If I should, replied the sailor, with perfect tranquillity, I hope, my Lord, I shall be able to bear it.

LETTER LXVIII.

Berlin.

Berlin is certainly one of the most beautiful cities in Europe. The streets are built in a very regular manner, and of a commodious breadth. In the new town they are perfectly straight. Frederick-street is reckoned two English miles and a half, or a French league, in length. Others which go off at right angles from that, are a mile, or a mile and a half long.

Some people assert, that Berlin covers as much ground as Paris. These are not Frenchmen, as you will readily believe; neither am I of that opinion, but it certainly approaches much nearer to Paris in size than in number of inhabitants; Berlin is undoubtedly more than half the size of Paris, yet I am convinced it does not contain above a fifth of the inhabitants.

There are a few very magnificent buildings in this town. The rest are neat houses, built of a fine white free-stone, generally one, or at most two stories high. Here, as at Potsdam, the finishing within does not correspond with the elegance of the outside, and the soldiers are quartered on the ground-floor in rooms looking to the street. The principal edifices are the King's palace, and that of Prince Henry. Both of these are very magnificent. The arsenal, which is a noble structure, is built in the form of a square. We were informed, that at present it contains arms for 200,000 men. I am convinced this is no exaggeration.

The new Roman Catholic church is by far the most elegant place of worship in the city. The King allows the free exercise of every religion over all his dominions. He thinks the smallest controul over men's consciences highly unjust. He even has the delicacy not to influence them by his example, and offends no religion, by giving a preference to any one in particular.

On the front of the opera-house, which is a very beautiful structure, is this inscription:

FREDERICUS REX, APOLLINI ET MUSIS.

After observing the inscriptions and ornaments of the palaces and other public buildings, the new method of decorating the churches, the number of Mercuries, Apollos, Minervas, and Cupids, that are to be met with in this country, a stranger might be led to suspect, that the Christian religion was exploded from the Prussian dominions, and old Jupiter and his family restored to their ancient honours.

There is an equestrian statue of William, the Great Elector, on the new bridge over the Spree. This is highly esteemed as a piece of fine workmanship.—In the corner of one of the squares, is a statue of Marshal Schwerin. He is represented holding the ensign with which he advanced at the famous battle of Prague.—Perceiving his troops on the point of giving way, he seized this from the officer's hands whose duty it was to carry it, and marched towards the enemy, calling out, Let all but cowards follow me. The troops, ashamed to abandon their general, charged once more, and turned the fortune of the day.—But the brave old Marshal was killed, in the eighty-fourth year of his age.—Do not you think the trouble of living so long was amply repaid by such a death?

Instead of saints or crucifixes, the King intends, that the churches of Berlin shall be ornamented with the portraits of men who have been useful to the state. Those of the Marshals Schwerin, Keith, Winterfield, and some others, are already placed in the great Lutheran church.

The society into which strangers may be admitted in this capital, is not various or extensive. The Prussian officers of the higher ranks, whose time is not entirely engrossed, like that of their inferiors, by the duties of their profession, live mostly with their own families, or with each other. Exclusive of other reasons which might determine them to this, it is understood, that the King does not approve of their forming intimacies with foreign ministers, or with strangers.

The D—— of H—— followed the King to Magdeburg to see the reviews there, and has since made a tour as far as Leipsic, with two English gentlemen. My connection with him, and the letter I brought from the Duchess of Brunswick, have procured me invitations, which I should otherwise have had but a small chance of receiving. I passed a day lately at a very pleasant villa, about six miles from Berlin, belonging to the King's brother, Prince Ferdinand. He is married to a sister of the Princess of Hesse Cassel's. The Princess of Prussia was there at the same time, and Prince Frederick of Brunswick, with his Princess, who is remarkably pretty. I have the honour of supping sometimes with Prince Frederick, who lives constantly at Berlin. To the spirit and vivacity common to all his family, he adds a taste for poetry, and has composed some dramatic pieces in the French language, which have been represented on a little theatre in his own house, and in private societies at Berlin.—There has been a continued round of feasting all the last week.

The Princess of Prussia gave a breakfast at a garden in the Park, to which a large company was invited. There was dancing, which continued all the forenoon. Upon all these occasions, I saw none of that state and ceremony of which the Germans are accused. Those of the highest rank behaved with the greatest ease and affability to every person present, and joined in the country-dances, without observing any form or etiquette.

The minister, Count Finkenstein, gave a great dinner and ball, on account of the marriage of one of his sons. The Count Reuse, and some others, have also given entertainments; but the chief and permanent society is to be found at the houses of the foreign ministers who reside here. I have been introduced to all of them by Mr. Harris, his Majesty's envoy extraordinary, who lives here in a style which does honour to his country and himself.

We have received very great civilities also from Baron Van Swieten, minister from, the Court of Vienna, a man of wit and erudition. He is son to the celebrated physician, whose works are so highly esteemed all over Europe. There are two or three general officers who are pretty often at the houses of these ministers, and entertain strangers occasionally at home.—Besides those I have named, there are very few of the King of Prussia's servants who have any connection with the strangers that come to Berlin. I have had the happiness of forming an acquaintance here with two very agreeable French gentlemen, the Marquis de Laval, son of the Duke of that name, and the Comte de Clermont, grandson of that Mons. de Saint Hillaire, whose arm was carried off by the same bullet which killed Marshal Turenne. You remember the sentiment which St. Hillaire expressed to his son, who lamented his wound—A sentiment which proved, that his magnanimity was equal to that of the hero whom he so greatly preferred to himself.

Adieu.

LETTER LXIX.

Berlin.

When we arrived here first, the Queen lived at Mont Bijou, a small palace just without the gates. Her Majesty had a public day twice a week while she remained there; but she has lately removed to Shoenhausen, another palace, situated two leagues from Berlin, where she passes the summer. Here she has a public day only once a week. The Princes, the nobility, the foreign ministers, and strangers, generally attend on these occasions at five in the evening. After her Majesty has walked round the circle, and spoke a few words to every one, she sits down to cards. There is a table for the Queen, and one for each of the Princesses, all of whom choose their own parties. The rest of the company present themselves for a few minutes at each of these card-tables, after which the duty of the day is over, and they walk in the garden, or form parties at cards in the other apartments, as they think proper, and return to Berlin when it begins to grow dark. On some particular nights, her Majesty invites a considerable number of the company to supper, who then remain till midnight.

The Queen's Court resembles the other Courts of Europe; whereas that at Sans-Souci is upon quite a new plan. No strangers are received there, nor any other persons, except such as have real business with the King. There his Majesty is employed in his affairs from morning till evening, and spends the hours he destines for relaxation in the company of two or three men of letters, and a few officers, who dine with him daily.—When he has business with any of his servants, or with the foreign ministers, which cannot be executed by letter, they attend him at Sans-Souci, and come away as soon as that business is transacted.

Those assemblies at Shoenhausen are the only established amusement for the ladies of quality at Berlin during the summer; but you have frequent opportunities of meeting with the court ladies at the houses of the foreign ministers.

The French manners and turn of thinking certainly prevail very little among the Prussian officers; but the ladies of the court of Berlin have more the air of French women, than those of any court I have seen. Mademoiselle de Hartfield, first lady of honour to the Queen, with an infinite deal of wit, has all the ease and elegance which distinguish the ladies of the Court of Versailles.

His Majesty very seldom appears at the Queen's court, or at any place where women form part of the assembly. When he inclines to unbend, his amusements are of a nature in which they can take no share. I once said to a lady of this Court, that it was a pity his Majesty did not love women.——Considering his time of life, said she, we could dispense with his love, but it is hard that he cannot endure us.

Notwithstanding this humour of the King's, the ladies here are by no means neglected by the men in general. Many of the married women particularly, have avowed admirers, who attend them on all occasions, are invited with them to all entertainments, sit next them at table, and whom the master or mistress of the feast takes care to place in the same party with them at cards. When a lady is not provided with an attendant of this kind, her husband, as well as herself, is generally a little out of countenance, and both seem rather in an aukward situation, till this necessary concomitant be found.

A misfortune of a very serious nature happened lately to a certain gentleman here; instead of expressing concern about him or his wife (for he was a married man), every body sympathized, in the tenderest manner, with another lady, between whom and this unfortunate gentleman the most intimate connection was thought to subsist: they said she was one of the worthiest women in the world, and of such delicate feelings, that her health might be injured by the impression the gentleman's misfortune would make upon her mind—Being surprised that no mention was made of his wife all this time, I asked if she might not also be in some measure affected by her husband's disaster?—I was told, that she was otherwise occupied, and that any thing which could happen to her husband was of little or no importance to her, I then enquired if she and her husband lived on bad terms; I was informed, that, on the contrary, they were on the best footing in the world, for that he was much attached to another woman—(the very lady they so greatly lamented) and that his wife was entirely devoted to another man; so the account between them being perfectly balanced, they lived free of all domestic debates, in a state of mutual neglect, and engrossed with separate passions.

In this country, when both parties are willing, and when there are no children, a divorce may be obtained with very little trouble or expence; we are frequently in companies, where a lady, her present, and former husband are at table, and all parties behave in the most polite and friendly manner to each other.

I have heard of one gentleman, who having lived in a state of domestic jarring with his wife, got her persuaded to concur with him in applying for a divorce.—This was soon obtained.—He then married another woman, with whom he was violently in love, and expected, as usual, eternal happiness. After marriage, however, this passion cooled rather sooner than common, and within a few months he became the professed admirer of his first wife. He now saw a thousand charms in her person and conversation, which had entirely escaped his notice, while the bonds of wedlock subsisted. He also discovered that certain peculiarities in her manner, which he had formerly thought exceedingly aukward, were in reality graceful. He expressed his remorse for his former blindness in the most pathetic terms: the lady was softened, and at length gave the most perfect marks of forgiveness; and it was universally thought, that he thus contrived to live in adultery with the very woman to whom he had been lawfully married.

Here jealousy is held in equal contempt and detestation, and scandal is very little known. People seem so fully occupied with their own private affairs, that they seldom trouble their heads about the business of their neighbours. If, in the course of conversation, an intimacy of a particular kind is hinted at between people of different sexes, it is mentioned accidentally as a fact of no importance, and without the smallest blame or ill-natured reflection on either of the parties. One reason of this may be, that there is scarce such a thing (I am assured) as an old maid in his Prussian Majesty's dominions.

The most fashionable walk in Berlin, is in the middle of one of the principal streets.—Before the houses on each side there is a causeway, and between these two causeways are fine gravel walks, planted with lime-trees.—Tents are pitched under these, and ice, lemonade, and other refreshments sold. The bands of music belonging to the regiments practise here in the summer.— The Company generally are in the greatest number in the evening, and often walk till it is very late.

———Nunc et campus, et areæ

Lenesque sub noctem susurri,

Composita repetantur hora.

LETTER LXX.

Nothing surprised me more, when I first came to Berlin, than the freedom with which the people spoke of the measures of government, and the conduct of the King. I have heard political topics, and others which I should have thought still more ticklish, discussed here with as little ceremony as at a London coffee-house. The same freedom appears in the booksellers' shops, where literary productions of all kinds are sold openly. The pamphlet lately published on the division of Poland, wherein the King is very roughly treated, is to be had without difficulty, as well as other performances, which attack some of the most conspicuous characters with all the bitterness of satire.

A government, supported by an army of 180,000 men, may safely disregard the criticisms of a few speculative politicians, and the pen of the satirist. While his Majesty retains the power of disposing of the lives and properties of his subjects as his wisdom shall direct, he allows them the most perfect freedom to amuse themselves with as many remarks or jokes on his conduct as they please.

The mind of this monarch is infinitely superior to that gossiping disposition, by which the despicable race of whisperers and retailers of scandal thrive at some courts. Convinced that the same perfidy, which can betray a real conversation, may invent a false one, he listens to no little, malicious tales of what has passed in private companies, or during the hours of convivial mirth. Any person who should attempt to repeat anecdotes of this kind to him, would be driven from his presence with disgrace. He treats with equal contempt all anonymous letters, and every kind of injurious information, when the informer declines appearing openly in support of his assertions.

This great Prince is so perfectly devoid of suspicion and personal fear, that he resides at Sans-Souci without any guard whatever. An orderly serjeant, or corporal only, attends there in the day-time to carry occasional orders to the garrison at Potsdam, whither he always returns in the evening. In this house, where the King sleeps every night, there are not above ten or a dozen persons, the servants included. When you recollect that Sans-Souci is a solitary mansion, about half a league from Potsdam, where all the guards are shut up, and therefore could be of no manner of use, in case of any attempt on the King's person during the night; when you consider that he, who lies thus defenceless and exposed, is a despotic monarch, who governs by the dictates of his own will and understanding, without minding the ill-humour or discontent of any man, or any set of men, and who, no doubt, has many inveterate enemies, you must confess, that all these circumstances argue great magnanimity.

Berlin, though not a fortified, is certainly a very military town. When all the soldiers of the garrison are present, they amount to 30,000. In their general conduct they are quiet, and the police of the town is pretty well regulated. Yet there are some kinds of irregularities which prevail in the highest degree. Public courtezans are more numerous here than in any town in Europe, in proportion to the number of inhabitants. They appear openly at the windows in the day-time, beckon to passengers as they walk in the streets, and ply for employment in any way they please, without disturbance from the magistrate.

It seems to be a received opinion here, that the peace and happiness of the community are not interrupted by this species of licentiousness; or perhaps it is believed, that an attempt to restrain it would be attended with consequences worse than the thing itself. Therefore nobody is allowed to molest or abuse those who have chosen this for a trade, and as little attention is paid to customers, who frequent the chambers of those ladies, as if they stept into any other house or shop, to purchase any other commodity.

Another species of debauchery is said to prevail in this capital.—I imagine, however, that what is related on that nauseous subject is greatly exaggerated.

The better kind of citizens and manufacturers live entirely among those of their own rank, and without affecting the manners of the courtiers, or stooping to the mean debauchery of the commonalty, maintain the decency, plainness, and honesty of the German character.

His Prussian Majesty has applied his attention to no object with so much zeal, and so little success, as to the establishing of commerce in his dominions. All his efforts, in order to this, have been rendered abortive by injudicious taxes, by monopolies, and other restrictions. Commerce, like the wild commoners of the air and the forest, when confined or shackled, immediately droops and dwindles, or, being alarmed, like Love,

"—— —— —— at sight of human ties,

Spreads its light wings, and in a moment flies."

LETTER LXXI.

I thank you, Sir, for the poem and pamphlets you sent me by ——. I own I do not think the former a very capital performance; yet am not surprised at the great run it has had. For though it had contained still a smaller proportion of wit, it would have been a good deal relished on account of the malignity and personal abuse with which it abounds.

The English nation have always had a great appetite for political writings; but those who cater for them have of late served up such messes of mere politics, as seem at length to have turned their stomachs. A little wit or personal satire is now found necessary to make even a newspaper go down. The first is not always at the command of the caterer: he therefore uses the other in its place, which answers his purpose as well.

I never had any delight in contemplating or exposing the dark side of human nature; but there are some shades so obvious, that you cannot open your eyes without observing them. The satisfaction that many people enjoy in reading libels, wherein private characters are traduced, is of that number. If to be abused in pamphlets and news-papers is considered as adversity, the truth of Rochefoucault's maxim is uncontrovertible:—Dans l'adversité de nos meilleurs amis, nous trouvons toujours quelquechose qui ne nous déplait pas.

The common scribblers of the age have turned to their own account this malevolent disposition, which they perceive to be so prevalent among men.—Like the people who provide bulls and other animals to be baited by dogs for the amusement of the spectators, these gentlemen turn out a few characters every week to be mangled and torn in the most cruel manner in the public news-papers.

It is the savage taste of those who pay for these amusements, which keeps them in use. The writers of scurrilous books in London often bear no more malice to the individuals they abuse, than the people at Paris and Vienna, who provide the other horrid amusement, bear to the boars, bulls, and other animals which they expose to the fury of dogs.

As for the scribblers, they seldom have any knowledge of the persons whose characters they attack. It is far from being impossible, that the author of the severe verses you sent me, has no more acquaintance with the lords and gentlemen against whom he writes with such bitterness, than the weaver who wove their pocket-handkerchiefs. The motive for the fabrication of the one as well as the other commodity most probably was daily bread, and this poetaster has preferred satire to panegyric, merely because he knew the first was most to the taste of his customers.

I remember once to have been in a certain bookseller's shop, when a letter was delivered to him, inclosing a paper, which, after he had thrown his eyes over it, he presented to me, telling me it was a character of Lord S——, which he intended to insert in a certain work then publishing.—I fancy, added he, it will do pretty well; the author is a sharp blade, I assure you;—none of my boys carry such an edge, or cut so deep, as that little gladiator.

I found this a most bitter invective against the above-mentioned nobleman, written with all the inveteracy of malice and personal enmity, branding him as a prodigy of sensuality, and accusing him of every villanous disposition and propensity that ever tainted the most corrupt heart.

This, said I, is a much more harmless production than is intended. The violence of this poison will prove its own antidote. The most voracious stomach for slander and defamation will not be able to bear such a dose, but must reject it with disgust. Every reader of common understanding will clearly perceive, that all this abuse has been dictated by malice and personal resentment.

Then, replied the bookseller, every reader of common understanding will clearly perceive what does not exist; for the writer of that paper, to my certain knowledge, never had the smallest intercourse or connection with Lord S———; never bore him any ill-will, and has not the most distant wish to injure that noble Lord; as a proof of which, added he, taking another paper out of his drawer, here is a character of the same nobleman, written by the same author, which is to appear about a week after the publication of the former, by way of answer to it.

This second paper was a continued eulogium on Lord S—— from beginning to end, in which the candid author, having compared him to some of the greatest and most celebrated men, and having collected many of the brightest flowers, with which Plutarch has adorned his worthies, he forms them into one large wreath, which he very seriously binds round the English nobleman's brow, concluding with this observation. That as his Lordship resembled them in their virtues, so like them he had been distinguished by the most virulent attacks of envy and malice, which was a tax that had always been paid for superior talents.

How comes my Lord S——, said I to the bookseller, to be selected from his brethren of the peerage, and distinguished so remarkably by the obloquy and the praise of your ingenious friend?

Because, replied he, that nobleman is at the head of an active department, and is one of those vigorous and decisive characters, which never fail to create a number of enemies and of friends. His enemies are delighted to see him abused, and it is expected, that his friends will be charmed to hear him praised; and, between the two, my friend's productions will find a brisk sale, and I hope to make a tolerable job of his Lordship; which, let me tell you, cannot be done with every man of rank.—Lord, Sir! there are some of them of such mawkish, water-gruel characters, as to interest no mortal. There is — —, a man of such high rank and such a known name, that I thought something might have been made of him:—And so I employed my little Drawcansir for and against him, and two very pretty pamphlets he produced;—but just as I was going to send them to the press, I happened to shew them to a friend of mine, who is an admirable judge in these matters.— These pamphlets, says he, are very well wrote; but they'll never pay the printing. The person who is the subject of them is of such a cold, tame, civil, cautious disposition, and has balanced so exactly through the whole of his life, that he has never obliged or disobliged any one. He has neither friend nor foe in the world:—Every body says, he is a good enough sort of a man; but were he to break his neck to-night, no human creature would feel either sorrow or satisfaction at the event, and a satire or panegyric on his grandmother would be as much read as those written on him.

In faith, sir, concluded the Bookseller, I took the hint, and so the pamphlets never appeared.

Though I was a good deal entertained with my friend the Bookseller's reasoning, yet I could not help feeling indignation at the literary bravo, who lived in this infamous manner, by wounding and murdering, or at least attempting to murder, people's reputations. And those are not entirely free from blame, who detesting the writer, take pleasure in the writings. He has very possibly the plea of necessitous circumstances to urge in alleviation of his wickedness:—but the pleasure they take seems to proceed from a pure, disinterested fondness of seeing others abused. Many of those who cry shame on the licentiousness of the press, and exclaim against the injustice and cruelty of tearing private characters to pieces in public papers, have the most virulent of these productions served up every morning as regularly as their toast and butter. If they would forego the pleasure of reading the most malicious of those compositions, the evil they complain of would cease directly.

But it is ridiculous, and seems ungrateful, for people to affect an appearance of indignation against those who provide for them one of the greatest enjoyments of their lives. To chuckle over scandal all the forenoon with every mark of pleasure, and decry it in the evening with affected anger, is as preposterous as it would be in a judge, first to seduce a poor wench to fornication, and then punish her for the sin.

You may possibly retort upon me, by putting me in mind of the admiration I expressed of the style of certain celebrated letters, wherein some eminent characters are dissected, and tortured with the scientific skill of an anatomist, and the refined cruelty of an inquisitor. I answer, that I admired the wit and genius, but not the disposition displayed in those letters.

Malice, when introduced by genius and wit, is often tolerated on account of the respect due to the introducers; but when the wretch comes alone, or is accompanied by dulness, which often happens, she will be expelled with infamy from all good company.

LETTER LXXII.

Berlin.

The Prussian army at present, according to my information, consists of 180,000 men. If twenty, or even thirty thousand are deducted from this account, on the supposition that it is exaggerated, still the remainder will be very great; and the expence of such an establishment in time of peace, seems to many almost incompatible with the King of Prussia's resources. Although the revenues of this monarch are much greater than is generally imagined, yet the armies he has supported, and continues to support; the palace he has built, and other expensive undertakings which he has completed, are not such proofs of the greatness of his revenue, as of the prudence with which it has been managed. Many other Princes have greater revenues, which, like water spilt on uncultivated land, and assisting the growth of useless weeds, are dissipated without taste or magnificence on the trumpery of a court and their dependents. Perhaps it was never known what miracles, œconomy, and assiduity through all the departments of government could perform, till this monarch made it apparent.

In the King of Prussia's dominions, there are none of those polls which enrich individuals at the expence of the public; places suited to the abilities and the luxury of the great, where the salary is large, because the application and talents requisite are small. If those who hold the most lucrative places in this court, can support a becoming dignity by the emoluments of their office, and lay up a very moderate provision for their families, it is the utmost they ever expect.

All commodities are highly taxed in the Prussian dominions. At Berlin, though money is a great deal scarcer than at London or Paris, a stranger will find very little difference in the ordinary expence of living. There are no means by which his revenue can be augmented, which this King has not tried. He has taxed even the vanity of his subjects, and drawn considerable supplies since the beginning of his reign from that plentiful source. The rage which the Germans, above all men, have for titles, prompts many of the wealthy citizens to purchase that of some office about court; and although the King employs no person void of abilities, he never scruples to permit this kind of traffic. The title, however, is literally all that is sold, for with regard to the real business of the office, the purchaser has as little connection with it after the bargain as before. Though his Majesty scarcely ever consults with any body, he has more nominal privy-counsellors than any King in Christendom.

The taxes in general are invariably fixed; but methods are found of drawing contributions from the proprietors of the very great estates, which do not affect the smaller landlords, or the rest of the subjects. The spirit of the government is not favourable to great and independent Lords. But both the great and the small landlords are prevented from squeezing or oppressing the peasants. As the soldiery are drawn from them, care is taken that they shall not be deprived of the chief source of health and vigour, and there is no peasantry in Europe better fed than the Prussian.

The army is chiefly composed of provincial regiments. The whole Prussian dominions being divided into circles or cantons; in each of these, one or more regiments, in proportion to the size and populousness of the division, have been originally raised, and from it the recruits continue to be taken; and each particular regiment is always quartered, in the time of peace, near the canton from which its recruits are drawn.

Whatever number of sons a peasant may have, they are all liable to be taken into the service except one, who is left to assist in the management of the farm. The rest wear badges from their childhood, to mark that they are destined to be soldiers, and ready to serve when the state requires them. If a peasant has only one son, he is not forced into the service, except he has the misfortune to be uncommonly stout and well-made. The King, however, endeavours to save his own peasantry, and draw as many recruits as he can from other countries:—For this purpose, there are Prussian officers employed at Hamburgh, Frankfort, and other free towns of Germany. I have seen them also at Neufchatel, and at places near French garrisons, attempting to inlist men, and pick up deserters. The recruits procured in this manner, remain continually with the regiments in which they are placed; but the native Prussians have every year eight or nine months of furlough, during which they return to their fathers' or brothers' houses, and work at the business of the farm, or gain their livelihood in any other way they please. Here is at once an immense saving in the expence of the army, and a great gain to the state from the labour of so many men.

From this it appears, that the Prussian army is neither more nor less than a standing militia, embodied for two or three months every year, and then dispersed to their usual labours as farmers.

I think this decides our old dispute on the subject of standing armies and militia. I expert therefore that you will, by the return of post, fairly and candidly acknowledge that I was in the right, and that all your arguments to prove, that a militia could not be depended on in the time of actual service, are built on false principles, and that my opinion was just and well-founded.

Before closing this letter, I will inform you of a very singular incident, the circumstances of which I relate, not so much with a design to illustrate the character or sentiments of the vulgar of this place in particular, as to furnish you with a curious fact in the history of human nature in general.

I went a few days since with Mr. F—— to see a man executed for the murder of a child.—His motives for this horrid deed were much more extraordinary than the action itself. He had accompanied some of his companions to the house of a fellow, who assumed the character of a fortune-teller, and having disobliged him, by expressing a contempt of his art, the fellow, out of revenge, prophesied, that this man should die on a scaffold.—This seemed to make little impression at the time, but afterwards recurred often to this unhappy creature's memory, and became every day more troublesome to his imagination. At length the idea haunted his mind so incessantly, that he was rendered perfectly miserable, and could no longer endure life.

He would have put himself to death with his own hands, had he not been deterred by the notion, that God Almighty never forgave suicide; though, upon repentance, he is very ready to pardon every other crime. He resolved, therefore, to commit murder, that he might be deprived of life by the hands of justice; and mingling a sentiment of benevolence with the cruelty of his intention, he reflected, that if he murdered a grown person, he might possibly send a soul to hell. To avoid this, he determined to murder a child, who could not have committed any sin which deserved damnation, but dying in innocence, would go immediately to Heaven. In consequence of these ideas, he actually murdered an infant of his master's, for whom he had always shewn an uncommon degree of fondness. Such was the strange account which this infatuated creature gave on his trial;—and thus the random prophecy proved, as in many other cases, the cause of its own completion.

He was executed about two miles from Berlin. As soon as he ascended the scaffold, he took off his coat and waistcoat;—his shirt was rolled down below his shoulders;—his night-cap was pulled over his eyes;—he was placed on his knees, and the executioner with a single stroke of a broad sword severed his head from his body.—It was the first time this executioner had performed:—there were two others of the same trade on the scaffold, who exhibited an instance of insensibility more shocking than the execution.— While the man's head rolled on the scaffold, and the arteries of the trunk poured out their blood, those men, with the gayest air you can imagine, shook their brother by the hand, wished him joy, and clapped him on the back, congratulating him on the dexterous and effectual manner in which he had performed his office.

LETTER LXXIII.

The D—— of H—— having expressed an inclination to visit the court of Mecklenburg Strelitz, I accompanied him thither soon after his return from Magdeburg and Leipsic. The weather being sultry, his Grace thought that travelling in the night would be most agreeable. We did not set out therefore till about six or seven in the evening. The first post-house is four German miles from Berlin; but as great part of the road is through a large wood, and the night became very dark, the postillions lost their way. In a short time we were perfectly bewildered, and without the smallest notion which direction we should follow. After many ineffectual attempts to find out the path, we thought it would be most prudent to unyoke the horses, and allow them to graze around, while we slept in the chaise till daybreak. This plan was literally followed: as soon as the servants, by the light of the rising sun, had discovered the path, we proceeded by Oranienburg and Seidneek to Reinsburg, which is a magnificent castle belonging to Prince Henry of Prussia.

The gardens here are very extensive, and have been highly improved and ornamented by this Prince, who has a good taste, and a magnificent turn of mind.

When we arrived at the town of New Strelitz, we were informed that the court was at Brandenburg. The Ducal residence was formerly at Old Strelitz; but the palace there, with all the magnificent furniture and effects, was burnt to ashes about fifty years ago. The fire having broke out in the night-time, the family themselves had a very narrow escape.

A new palace has been since built at the distance of two English miles from where the former stood, but in a much more agreeable situation, being placed on a gentle eminence near a fine lake; and the town of New Strelitz has gradually arisen in the neighbourhood.

After a short stay at Strelitz, we proceeded to New Brandenburg, which is some leagues farther north, and within a small distance of the Baltic. We arrived there in the morning of the third day after we had left Berlin. When the Chamberlain of the Court was informed of the D—— of H——'s arrival, we received an invitation to dinner, and a coach and equipage were ordered to attend his Grace.

The reigning Duke of Mecklenburg Strelitz is unmarried, as well as the Princess, his sister, who lives constantly with him. They are both of a darker complexion than the Queen of Great Britain, and neither of them so tall; nor have they much external resemblance of her Majesty, except in the affability of their manner. The Duke is beloved by his subjects, on account of the humanity and benevolence of his disposition, which seem to be characteristic of the whole family.—After dinner there was a concert of music, and card-playing till supper.

The whole country of Mecklenburg was for many centuries under the government of one Prince. In the year 1592, on the death of the Sovereign, it was divided between his two sons. The eldest retaining the Duchy of Mecklenburg Schwerin, which is considerably the largest share; the younger obtained the Duchy of Mecklenburg Strelitz. This last branch became extinct in the year 1695, and Duke Frederic William, of the eldest branch, laid claim to the inheritance of the Duchy of Strelitz. But he was opposed by Adolphus Frederic, his father's younger brother, and the contest was settled by compromise between the parties in 1701. The right of primogeniture, and the lineal succession, were then established in both houses, and this final agreement was ratified by the Emperor.

The country here is not a sandy flat, as around Berlin; but the soil becomes gradually better as you move from that city, and around New Brandenburg it is remarkably fertile. Though the southern border of this Duchy is flat, sandy and barren, yet all the northern part is of a rich verdure, finely diversified with hills, meadows, woods, and several beautiful lakes from four to ten miles in length. The country yields plenty of corn, hemp, flax, excellent pasture for numerous flocks of sheep, and a good breed of horses.—New Brandenburg is a neat and thriving town, very agreeably situated. The inhabitants carry on a considerable trade in hops, which grow in great abundance all around.

This country, which seems to be happy in its prince and other particulars, cannot rank among its blessings the neighbourhood of so great and warlike a monarch as the King of Prussia. In the course of the late war, both the Mecklenburgs suffered very severely from this circumstance. The Russians and Austrians, who pillaged the middle Mark of Brandenburg, did not ascertain with nicety where the King of Prussia's dominions ended, and the Duke of Strelitz's began; but as often as there was any thing valuable to carry away, plundered both without distinction. And when that Monarch himself was driven to extremity, and obliged to use every means of recruiting his army, the Mecklenburghers were cajoled and seduced by every art into the Prussian service; and when these methods failed, they were, as it is said, taken by force. Even at present, whenever the Prussian recruiting officers know of a strong well-looking peasant belonging to the Duchy of Mecklenburg, they use every means they can devise to seduce him into their master's service.— Complaints are frequently made of these practices to his Prussian Majesty, and redress will be given when it shall please the Lord.

The second day after our arrival, we spent the forenoon in viewing every thing worthy of notice in the town, and dined again at court, where there was a more numerous company than had been the first day. After dinner we accompanied his Highness and the Princess to an assembly in the town, and returned to sup at the court. During supper there was a concert of vocal and instrumental music.

Having received every mark of polite attention from this Prince, we took leave of him and the Princess, and left the town early next morning, and returned by Old Strelitz, which is not in such a flourishing condition, or situated in so fine a country, as New Brandenburg. While British subjects pass through this country, they will naturally reflect with gratitude and veneration on the character of a Princess whose virtues are an ornament to the British throne, and whose amiable manners and prudent conduct have united the affections of a people divided by party, and irreconcilable in sentiment on almost every other subject.

On our return to Berlin, I found a letter from Lord Marechal, informing me, that the King was expected at Potsdam within a very few days; that great preparations were making for the reception of the Princess of Hesse and the Duchess of Wurtemberg, who were then both at Berlin, and were to pay a visit to the King at Sans-Souci; that they would be accompanied by the Princess Amelia, the King's unmarried sister, and his two sisters-in-law, for all of whom apartments were preparing at the new palace, where his majesty also was to reside all the time that his illustrious guests should remain. My Lord added, that the celebrated Le Kain, and a company of French comedians, were already arrived, and also a company of Italian actors and singers for the opera; and that both companies were to perform at the theatre within the palace; that a great concourse of company was expected at Potsdam on the occasion; that most of the apartments in the town were already bespoke, and, as he imagined we should incline to be there, he had engaged lodgings for us.

The Duke was extremely pleased with this obliging behaviour of Lord Marechal. I afterwards spoke to Mr. Harris on this subject, and enquired if he intended to be at Potsdam on the occasion? He told me, that as the plays, operas, and other entertainments, were to be given in the palace, nobody could attend them except those who had particular invitations; that neither he nor any of the foreign ministers had been, or, as he understood, were to be invited, nor did he hear that any strangers were expected;—and that he imagined it would be unbecoming the D—— of H—— to be at Potsdam at that time, except he could with propriety attend the entertainments at Sans-Souci.

His Grace, on hearing this account, determined to remain here; but some days after, I received a letter from Count Finkenstein, acquainting me, that he had orders to invite the D—— of H—— and me to attend the entertainments to be given at Sans-Souci. This afforded us great satisfaction, not so much on account of the public entertainments, as because it will give us opportunities, which we could not otherwise have, of seeing the King of Prussia, and probably in an easier way than at Berlin. As for the usual amusements and splendor of courts, his Grace displays more coolness about them than one would naturally imagine, considering the manner in which he is received, his time of life, and his personal appearance.

——namque ipsa decoram

Cæsariem nato genitrix, lumenque juventæ

Purpureum, & lætos oculis afflarat honores.

Since our return from Mecklenburg, we have passed our time almost constantly with Mr. Harris, who accompanied the Duke yesterday on his last visit to Shoenhausen; for we shall probably not return to this place from Potsdam. Mr. F—— set out a few days ago for Frankfort on the Maine; his easy humour, and original turn of thought, make his absence felt with pain by all who have tasted the pleasure of his conversation.

Adieu.

LETTER LXXIV.

Potsdam.

We have been here about a fortnight. His Majesty arrived at the new palace of Sans-Souci about the same time that we came to Potsdam. The Princess Amelia, who is mistress of the ceremonies, was there to receive him. The company I formerly mentioned are all lodged in the palace, I will give you a short sketch of what has passed.

There has been a theatrical entertainment every second or third day. His Grace and I attend at Sans-Souci on these days only. We drive from Potsdam about five in the evening. The company assemble in one of the apartments of the palace about that time, and walk to the playhouse a little before six. The theatre is very well contrived for the accommodation of a small audience. There are neither boxes nor pit; but semicircular benches in the front of the stage. The foremost bench is upon the floor; the others rise gradually behind, that all the spectators may see equally well.

A few minutes after the company are placed, the Royal Family arrive. The Princess Amelia is led in by Prince Frederick of Brunswick, and the Princess of Hesse by the King. The Duchess of Wurtemberg, and the other Princesses, are led in after; they, and the ladies their attendants, sit in the first rows. The King generally seats himself in the third or fourth. The piece then begins, and is usually finished about nine, after which all the company return to the large apartment, where the King remains conversing in a familiar manner till supper is ready. He then retires, and goes to bed at ten.

Those whom the Princess Amelia orders to be invited, stay to supper; and there is generally a pretty numerous company.—We have been at this repast three or four times, and usually get to our lodgings at Potsdam about midnight.

Hitherto there have been no comedies acted, and I understand there are to be none, because Le Kain never acts in comedy; and for another reason, which is equivalent to a thousand,—his Majesty loves tragedy better.

Le Kain has already appeared in some of his principal characters.—You need not doubt of his exerting all his powers before such an audience.—I might have said, such an auditor. The King seemed pleased with his acting, and of consequence the courtiers were in raptures, and vied with each other who should praise him most.

The tragedy of Oedipus is his Majesty's favourite piece. This has been represented twice, and he seemed to enjoy it very much on both occasions; particularly when the following speech against priests was pronounced:

Tandis que par vos soins vous pouvez tout apprendre,

Quel besoin que le Ciel ici se fasse entendre?

Ces Dieux, dont le pontife a promis le secours,

Dans leus temples, Seigneur, n'habitent pas toujours;

On ne voit point leur bras si prodigue en miracles;

Ces antres, ces trépieds, qui rendent leurs oracles,

Ces organes d'airain que nos mains ont formés,

Toujours d'un souffle pur ne sont point animés.

Ne nous endormons point sur la foi de leurs prêtres;

Au pied du sanctuaire il est souvent des traîtres,

Qui nous asservissant sous un pouvoir sacré,

Font parler les destins, les font taire à leur gré.

Voyez, examinez, avec un soin extrême,

Philoctète, Phorbas, & Jocaste elle-même.

Ne nous fions qu'à nous, voyons tout par nos yeux,

Ce sont là nos trépieds, nos oracles, nos Dieux.

And afterwards, when Jocasta pours forth another tirade of the same kind, which terminates with these lines:

Nos Prêtres ne sont point ce qu'un vain peuple pense;

Notre crédulité fait toute leur science.

I happened to sit next to the Abbé Bastiani, and, while the actress spoke this, the king started up, coughed, and laughed, with very significant gestures, to the ecclesiastic.

But though these passages, and some others, seem at first sight to be severe against priests, the tragedy of Oedipus, upon the whole, does them great honour. For all that is said against them, turns out to be unjust, and it appears that the oracle, which had been treated in such severe terms, was true, and that the high priest had acted throughout like an honest and virtuous man. It surprises me, therefore, that Voltaire should have taken the plot of his play from the Greek tragedy on this subject, which has constrained him, like Balaam the son of Barak, to do honour to those whom he would have been better pleased to have cursed.—And the King on his part (if I may presume to say it) could not have pitched upon a tragedy less à-propos, if his intention was to turn the clergy into ridicule.

I have no objection to this piece, on account of the honour done to the clergy; because I cannot help forming an opinion of men from my own experience: And I have known so many good men of that profession, that I should respect it on their account, exclusive of other reasons.

But I own I have the misfortune not to follow this great monarch, and many other respectable critics, in their admiration of the tragedy of Oedipus.—The fable, in my poor opinion, is too horrible.—The circumstance of Oedipus being married to his mother, and having children by her, is highly disgusting; and the idea it gives of Providence and the conduct of the gods, cannot have a good effect on the mind. Nothing could be more unjust, than that Heaven should send a plague among the inhabitants of Thebes, and pour such vengeance on poor Oedipus and Jocasta, for crimes of which it knew them to be innocent. We cannot help admitting the justice of Oedipus's reproaches against the gods, when he says,

Le voilà donc rempli cet oracle exécrable,

Dont ma crainte a pressé l'effet inévitable:

Et je me vois enfin, par un mélange affreux,

Inceste, & parricide, & pourtant vertueux.

Miserable vertu, nom stérile & funeste,

Toi par qui j'ai réglé des jours que je déteste,

A mon noir ascendant tu n'as pû resister:

Je tombais dans le piége, en voulant l'éviter.

Un dieu plus fort que moi m'entraînait vers le crime;

Sous mes pas fugitifs il creusait un abîme;

Et j'etais, malgré moi, dans mon aveuglement,

D'un pouvoir inconnu l'esclave & l'instrument.

Voilà tous mes forfaits, je n'en connais point d'autres.

Impitoyables dieux, mes crimes sont les vôtres,

Et vous m'en punissez....

We must suspect, however, that Jocasta has mistaken in the opinion she utters in the concluding lines of the tragedy.

Prêtres, & vous Thébains, qui futes mes sujets,

Honorez mon bucher, & songez à jamais,

Qu'au milieu des horreurs du destin qui m'opprime,

J'ai fait rougir les dieux, qui m'ont forcée au crime.

For those, who could force innocent people to commit criminal actions, and then punish them on that account, were not capable of blushing for any thing. A French tragedy and Italian opera are represented at this theatre alternately; the King attends the latter as punctually as the former, and displays in his countenance that extreme sensibility to music, which forms part of his character. I imagine this Prince would succeed better in any thing than in simulation, if he should ever think it worth his while to attempt that part of hypocrisy,—his features are so expressive of his feelings, that the first would be constantly in danger of betraying the other. When there is no representation at the theatre, his Majesty has a private concert in his own apartment, where he himself performs on the German flute, in which instrument he has attained the highest degree of excellence.—To these concerts no stranger is admitted.

LETTER LXXV.

Potsdam.

When we first arrived here, there was nothing I was so eager to see as the Prussian troops at their exercise; but the reviews at Berlin have completely satiated my curiosity. And though the gardens of the palace are just opposite to the windows of our inn, I hardly ever go to look at the guards, who are paraded there every forenoon.—A few days ago, however, I happened to take a very early walk about a mile out of town, and seeing some soldiers under arms, in a field at a small distance from the road, I went towards them. An officer on horseback, whom I took to be the Major, for he gave the word of command, was uncommonly active, and often rode among the ranks to reprimand, or instruct, the common men. When I came nearer, I was much surprised to find that this was the king himself. He had his sword drawn, and continued to exercise the corps for an hour after. He made them wheel, march, form the square, and fire by divisions, and in platoons, observing all their motions with infinite attention; and, on account of some blunder, put two officers of the Prince of Prussia's regiment in arrest.—In short, he seemed to exert himself with all the spirit of a young officer, eager to attract the notice of his General by uncommon alertness.

I expressed my surprise to an officer present, that the King was not willing to take some repose, particularly from that kind of employment of which he had had so very much of late, and that he could take so much pains with a mere handful of men immediately after he had come from exercising whole armies.

This gentleman told me, that, on this particular day, the King had been trying some new evolutions; but though this had not been the case, he might very possibly have been in the field:—for his maxim was, that his troops should display as much briskness on a common field-day as if they were to engage in battle; and therefore it was never known when he intended to be present, or when not;—that as for repose, he took it between ten at night and four in the morning, and his other hours were all devoted to action, either of body or mind, or both; and that the exercise he had just taken, was probably by way of relaxation after three hours previous labour in his cabinet.

The more I see and hear of this extraordinary man, the more am I astonished. He reconciles qualities which I used to think incompatible. I once was of opinion, that the mind, which stoops to very small objects, is incapable of embracing great ones;—I am now convinced, that he is an exception; for while few objects are too great for his genius, none seem too small for his attention.

I once thought that a man of much vivacity was not capable of entering into the detail of business:—I now see that he, who is certainly a man of wit, can continue methodically the necessary routine of business, with the patience and perseverance of the greatest dunce that ever drudged in a compting-house.

Since my last, we have seen the Italians perform; but neither the plays nor the operas, nor any part of the entertainments, interest me half so much, or could draw me so assiduously to Sans-Souci, as the opportunity this attendance gives of seeing the King. Other monarchs acquire importance from their station; this Prince gives importance to his. The traveller in other countries has a wish to see the King, because he admires the kingdom:—here the object of curiosity is reversed:—and let us suppose the palaces, and the towns, and the country, and the army of Prussia ever so fine, yet our chief interest in them will arise from their belonging to Frederic the Second;—the man, who, without an ally but Britain, repelled the united force of Austria, France, Russia, and Sweden.

Count Nesselrode, talking with me on this subject, had an expression equally lively and just: C'est dans l'adversité qu'il brille, lorsqu'il est bien comprimé il a un ressort irrésistible.

The evening of the day on which I had seen the King in the field, I was at Sans-Souci; for I wish to neglect no opportunity of being present where this monarch is. I like to stand near him, to hear him speak, and to observe his movements, attitudes, and most indifferent actions. He always behaves with particular affability to the D—— of H——. One evening, before the play began, his Grace and I were standing accidentally with Count Finkenstein, in a room adjoining to the great apartment where the company were. The King entered alone, when he was not expected, and immediately began a conversation with the D——.

He asked several questions relating to the British constitution; particularly at what age a peer could take his seat in parliament?—When the Duke replied, At twenty-one.—It is evident from that, said the King, that the English Patricians acquire the necessary talents for legislation much sooner than those of ancient Rome, who were not admitted into the Senate till the age of forty.

He then enquired about the state of Lord Chatham's health, and expressed high esteem for the character of that minister.—He asked me, if I had received letters by the last post, and if they mentioned any thing of the affairs in America?—He said, there were accounts from Holland, that the English troops had been driven from Boston, and that the Americans were in possession of that place.—— I told him, our letters informed us, that the army had left Boston to make an attack with more effect elsewhere.

He smiled, and said—If you will not allow the retreat to have been an affair of necessity, you will at least admit, that it was *tout-à-fait à propos*.

He said he heard that some British officers had gone into the American service, and mentioned Colonel Lee, whom he had seen at his Court. He observed, that it was a difficult thing to govern men by force at such a distance;—that if the Americans should be beat (which appeared a little problematical), still it would be next to impossible to continue to draw from them a revenue by taxation;—that if we intended conciliation with America, some of our measures were too rough; and if we intended its subjection, they were too gentle. He concluded by saying, Enfin, Messieurs, je ne comprends pas ces choses là; je n'ai point de colonie:—j'espère que vous vous tirerez bien d'affaire, mais elle me parôit un peu épineuse.—— Having said this, he walked into the Princess's apartment, to lead her to the playhouse, while we joined the company already assembled there.—The tragedy of Mahomet was performed, which, in my opinion, is the finest of all Voltaire's dramatic pieces, and that in which Le Kain appears to the greatest advantage.

LETTER LXXVI.

Potsdam.

You express such an earnest desire to be made acquainted with every thing which regards the King of Prussia, that I am in danger of lengthening my descriptions with a tedious minuteness. Yet I will risk it, rather than give you reason to complain that I have not gratified your curiosity as fully as is in my power.

Do not imagine, however, that I presume to draw a complete portrait of this monarch. That must be the work of much abler painters, who have seen him in a more familiar manner, and whose colours can give an expression worthy of the original. I shall only attempt to give a faithful sketch of such features as I was able to seize during the transient views I myself had, or which I have learnt from those who have passed with him many of the hours which he dedicates to free conversation, and the pleasures of the table.

The King of Prussia is below the middle size, well made, and remarkably active for his time of life. He has become hardy by exercise and a laborious life; for his constitution originally seems to have been none of the strongest. His look announces spirit and penetration. He has fine blue eyes; and, in my opinion, his countenance upon the whole is agreeable. Some who have seen him are of a different opinion. All who judge from his portraits only, must be so; for although I have seen many which have a little resemblance of him, and some which have a great deal, yet none of them do him justice. His features acquire a wonderful degree of animation while he converses.—This is entirely lost upon canvas.

He stoops considerably, and inclines his head almost constantly to one side.

His tone of voice is the cleared and most agreeable in conversation I ever heard.

He speaks a great deal; yet those who hear him, regret that he does not speak a great deal more. His observations are always lively, very often just, and few men possess the talent of repartee in greater perfection.

He hardly ever varies his dress, which consists of a blue coat, lined and faced with red, and a yellow waistcoat and breeches. He always wears boots, with hussar tops, which fall in wrinkles about his ancles, and are oftener of a dark brown than a black colour.

His hat would be thought extravagantly large in England, though it is of the size commonly used by the Prussian officers of cavalry. He generally wears one of the large side corners over his forehead and eyes, and the front cock at one side.

He wears his hair cued behind, and dressed with a single buckle on each side. From their being very carelessly put up and unequally powdered, we may naturally conclude, that the friseur has been greatly hurried in the execution of his office.

He uses a very large gold snuff-box, the lid ornamented with diamonds, and takes an immoderate quantity of Spanish snuff, the marks of which very often appear on his waistcoat and breeches. These are also liable to be soiled by the paws of two or three Italian greyhounds, which he often caresses.

He dresses as soon as he gets up in the morning. This takes up but a few minutes, and serves for the whole day.—You have often heard that the King of Prussia's hours, from four or five in the morning, till ten at night, are all dedicated methodically to particular occupations, either of business or amusement. This is certainly true, and the arrangement has not sustained such an interruption for many years, as since the present company came to Potsdam.

Some who pretend to more than common penetration assert, that at present they can perceive marks of uneasiness in his countenance, and seem convinced, that there will not be such another company at Sans-Souci during this reign.

All business with the King is transacted by letters. Every petition or proposal must be made in this form, which is adhered to so invariably, as I have been assured, that if any of his Generals wished to promote a cadet to the rank of an ensign, he would not venture to make his proposal in any other manner, even though he had daily opportunities of conversing with his Majesty.

The meanest of his subjects may apply to him in writing, and are sure of an answer. His first business every morning is the perusing the papers addressed to him. A single word wrote with his pencil in the margin, indicates the answer to be given, which is afterwards made out in form by his secretaries.—This method affords the King time to deliberate on the justice and propriety of every demand, and prevents the possibility of his being surprised into a promise, which it might be inconvenient to perform.

He sits down to dinner precisely at noon. Of late he allows more time to this repast than formerly. It is generally after three before he leaves the company. Eight or nine of his officers are commonly invited to dine with him. Since our coming to Potsdam, Count Nesselrode, and the Abbé Bastiani, two men of letters, were the only company, besides the officers, who dined with the King, while he lived in his usual way at the Old Palace of Sans-Souci; and those two were then of his party almost every day. The Count has now left this Court; the Abbé has an apartment in the Palace. He is an Italian by birth, a man of wit, and an excellent companion.

At table, the King likes that every person should appear to be on a footing, and that the conversation should be carried on with perfect freedom. The thing, by the way, is impossible. That confidential unrestrained flow of the heart, which takes place in a society of equals, is a pleasure which a despotic Prince can never taste. However, his Majesty desires that it may be so, and they make the best of it they can.

At one of these meetings, when the King was in a gay humour, he said to Bastiani,—When you shall obtain the tiara, which your exemplary piety must one day procure you, how will you receive me when I arrive at Rome to pay my duty to your Holiness?—I will immediately give orders, replied the Abbé, with great readiness, Qu'on fasse entrer l'aigle noir,—qu'il me couvre de ses ailes, mais—qu'il m'épargne de son bec.

Nobody says more lively things in conversation than the King himself. Many of his bons mots are repeated here, I shall only mention one, which is at once an instance of his wit, and greatness of mind, in rendering justice to the merit of a man who has caused him more vexation than perhaps any other person alive.—When the King of Prussia had a personal meeting some years since with the Emperor; they always dined together, a certain number of their principal officers being with them. One day, General Laudohn was going to place himself at the bottom of the table, when the King, who was at the head, called to him, Venez, je vous en prie, Monsieur Laudohn, placez vous ici. J'aime infiniment mieux vous avoir de mon cotè que vis-à-vis.

Though all the cordiality of friendship, and the full charms of unreserved society, cannot exist where the fortune of every other individual depends on the will of one of the company; yet the King endeavours to put every one as much at his ease as the nature of the case will admit, and I have heard of his bearing some very severe retorts with perfect good humour. He has too much wit himself, and is too fond of it in others, to repel its attacks with any other weapons than those which it furnishes. None but the most absurd of dunces could attempt to rally, without being able to allow of raillery; and only the meanest of souls would think of revenging the liberties taken with a companion by the power of a King.

A very striking instance of the freedom which may be used with him occurred a little before the late reviews, and what makes it more remarkable, it happened, not during the gaiety of the table, but on the very scene of military strictness.

Two regiments were in the field. That of General —— was one of them. This officer is fond of company, and passes more of his time in the society of strangers, and with the foreign ministers, than most others in the Prussian service.—Something, it is probable, had chagrined the King that morning. While the regiment advanced in a line, he said to the General, who stood near him, Votre regiment n'est pas aligné, Monsieur ——, et ce n'est pas surprenant, vous jouez tant aux cartes. The General called out instantly with a loud voice to the regiment, Alte! and they immediately stopped: then, turning to the King, he said, Il n'est pas question, Sire, de mes cartes—Mais, ayez la bonté de regarder si ce regiment n'est pas aligné.—The regiment was in a very straight line, and the King moved away without speaking, and seemingly displeased, not with the General, but with himself.—This manly officer never had reason afterwards to believe that the King had taken his freedom amiss.

I have already said, that it is absolutely impossible for any man to enjoy an office in the King of Prussia's service without performing the duty of it. He is himself active and assiduous, and he makes it a point that all his ministers and servants shall be so too. But to those who know their business, and perform it exactly, he is an easy and equitable master.

A gentleman, who has been many years about his person, and is now one of his aid-de-camps, assured me of this:—The King understands what ought to be done: and his servants are never exposed to the ridiculous or contradictory orders of ignorance, or the mortifications of caprice.

His favourites, of whatever kind, never were able to acquire influence over him in any thing regarding business. Nobody ever knew better how to discriminate the merit of those who serve him in the important departments of state, from theirs who contribute to his amusement. A man who performs the duty of his office with alertness and fidelity, has nothing to apprehend from the King's being fond of the company and conversion of his enemy. Let the one be regaled at the King's table every day, while the other never receives a single invitation; yet the real merit of both is known:—and if his adversary should ever try to turn the King's favour to the purposes of private hatred or malice, the attempt will be repelled with disdain, and the evil he intended to another, will fall on himself.

LETTER LXXVII.

On the days when there is no public court at Sans-Souci, we generally dine with Lord Marechal, who is always happy to see the D—— of H——, and is of great service to all British subjects while they remain here or at Berlin. Exclusive of other reasons he may have for esteeming the Duke, his Lordship evidently displays a kind of partiality for his Grace, as the first man in point of rank belonging to his country. This appears in a thousand instances; for with very liberal sentiments, and a most benevolent heart, this venerable nobleman still retains a few Caledonian prejudices.

He asked one day of the D——, If he reckoned himself a Scotchman? Most certainly I do, replied his Grace. By so doing you lie under a mistake, said my Lord; for I can assure you, and I am convinced the best lawyers in England will do the same, that you have a much juster claim to all the privileges belonging to your English title of B——n, though some of them, I fear, are still disputed.

It is to be hoped, said the D——, that the House of Peers will not always refuse to do my family justice; on a thorough examination of the case, I still flatter myself they will grant me those privileges, which have been, for no valid reasons, refused my ancestors. But in the mean time, why will your Lordship, more cruel than the Peers, deny my birth-right as a Scotchman?

Because your birth gives you no such right, replied the Earl; for you in reality are but a North Briton:—unless your Grace can prove that you were born before the Union. But, continued he, with an air of triumph, I am a real Scotchman:—adding a little after, with a sigh, and in a plaintive accent—and almost the only one in the world—All the Scots of my acquaintance are now dead.

The good old Earl is infinitely fond of talking of his country, and of the days of former years. When I make any enquiry about the King of Prussia, or concerning Spain or Italy, in which countries he resided so long, he answers with a kind of complaisant brevity, and immediately turns the discourse back to Scotland, to which his heart seems wonderfully attached.

In the time of dinner, one of his servants, a stout highlander, generally entertains the company by playing on the bagpipe. I have observed, that these North Britons (to abide by Lord Marechal's distinction) who are the most zealous for the interest and honour of their country, and who value themselves on being born north of the Tweed, are particularly, if not exclusively, fond of this instrument. You will, at least, allow that your gallant friend, Lord E———n, is no exception to this observation; and perhaps you will admit, that it requires a considerable degree of patriotism, or *amor Caledoniæ* to have a great relish for the melody of a bagpipe.

I called on Lord Marechal one afternoon, just as the King had left him; for the monarch, without any form or previous notice, sometimes walks through the garden, and pays a short visit to his old friend, to whom he has an unalterable attachment, both from personal regard, and on account of the high estimation in which he holds the memory of his brother Marechal Keith.

Another day I was with the Earl, when the Princesses of Prussia and Hesse, with Prince Frederic of Brunswic, all entered and demanded coffee, which my Lord immediately ordered, with the addition of a couple of melons; telling the Princesses, he knew they would not stay long enough with a man of eighty, to give time for preparing a better repast.—Thus favoured by the monarch and the Princes, you will not doubt that the old Earl's friendship is cultivated by the rest of the court.

The Hereditary Prince of Prussia lives in a small house in the town of Potsdam. His appointments do not admit of that degree of magnificence, which might be expected in the Heir of the crown;—but he displays a spirit of hospitality far more obliging than magnificence; and doubly meritorious, considering the very moderate revenue allowed him. We generally sup there two or three times a week.

This Prince is not often of the King's parties, nor is it imagined that he enjoys a great share of his uncle's favour. In what degree he possesses the talents of a general is not known, as he was too young to have any command during the late war. But he certainly has a very just understanding, which has been improved by study. He has taken some pains to acquire the English language, to which he was induced by an admiration of several English authors, whose works he had read in French and German. He is now able to read English prose with tolerable facility, and has been of late studying Shakespear, having actually read two or three of his plays.

I took the liberty to observe, that as Shakespear's genius had traced every labyrinth, and penetrated into every recess of the human heart, his sentiments could not fail to please his Royal Highness; but, as his language was uncommonly bold and figurative, and full of allusions to national customs, and the manners of our island two centuries ago, the English themselves, who had not made a particular study of his works, did not always comprehend their full energy. I added, that to transfuse the soul of Shakespear into a translation, was impossible; and to taste all his beauties in the original, required such a knowledge of the English manners and language as few foreigners, even after a long residence in the capital, could attain.

The Prince said, he was aware of all this; yet he was determined to struggle hard for some acquaintance with an author so much admired by the English nation; that though he should never be able to taste all his excellencies, he was convinced he should understand enough to recompence him for his trouble; that he had already studied some detached parts, which he thought superior to any thing he had ever met with in the works of any other Poet. His Royal Highness attends to military business with as much assiduity as most officers of the same rank in the army; for in the Prussian service, no degree of eminence in the article of birth can excuse a remission in the duties of that profession. He is much esteemed by the army, and considered as an exceeding good officer. To the frankness of a soldier he joins the integrity of a German, and is beloved by the public in general, on account of his good-nature, affability, and humane turn of mind.

LETTER LXXVIII.

I am afraid you will think the anecdotes and conversation which I sometimes send you are rather tedious. Your curiosity about certain characters has led me into this practice; for I choose to give you opportunities of forming an opinion of your own, rather than to trouble you with mine. My opinion might very probably be erroneous; the accounts I give of what I have seen or heard are always true. And, notwithstanding that the actions and conversations I relate, may be apparently of small importance, still as the persons in some measure describe themselves, an understanding like yours will be able from thence to draw juster ideas of character than I could have given.

In a former letter I mentioned the great difficulty of deserting from a Prussian garrison, and of what importance it is thought to prevent it. An incident which happened a few days since, will give you a stronger idea of this than any general account.

Two soldiers of the Prince of Prussia's regiment got over the walls in the night-time, with an intention to desert; but unluckily for them, this town stands on a peninsula formed by the river, and the neck of land is guarded in such a manner that it is almost impossible to pass that way without permission. These men could not swim, and they durst not present themselves at any of the ferries, because the boatmen are forbid, under the severest penalties, to connive at the escape of any deserters, and strictly ordered to assist in apprehending them. A reward is also offered, as a greater inducement to this piece of service.

All these circumstances being known in the garrison, it was imagined that, as none of the peasants would in all probability venture to harbour them, they were still skulking in the fields among the standing corn. On this supposition, parties of men were employed for three days successively in traversing the fields, and beating the bushes, as if they had been in chace of a hare. Great numbers of the officers of this regiment, some of the highest rank, rode about for three or four hours every day, all employed in the same manner. But not finding the men, they were at last convinced that they had by some means or other got out of the peninsula, and all further search was given up as unnecessary.

On the morning of the fourth day, these two unfortunate men came and surrendered to the guard at one of the gates. Finding it impracticable to effect their escape, and not daring to enter a house, they were at length compelled by hunger and fatigue to deliver themselves up.

Before I close this letter, I will give you an account of an adventure of an affecting nature, which happened in the King's family, at the time when all these researches were made for the two deserters.

The King's principal valet-de chambre was a man considerably respected. Having constant opportunities of being about the King's person, and having enjoyed his approbation for several years, people of the first rank paid him some degree of attention. He was liked by his acquaintances, as I have been told, on account of his personal qualities, and had accumulated a little fortune by the perquisites of his office. He had built a house near that of my Lord Marechal, and kept a coach for the use of his mistress.

It was this man's misfortune to disoblige the King, probably by some neglect of duty; or it might possibly be something worse:—I never could hear exactly how this had happened:—But while the Princesses were at the New Palace, the King had blamed him in very sharp terms; and not being satisfied with the excuses the man made, he told him, that, as soon as the company was gone, he should be taken care of.

When the Princesses went to Berlin, his Majesty returned to his old palace at Sans-Souci; and the day after, he sent for an officer of his guards, and ordered him to conduct this man to Potsdam, and place him in the quality of a drummer in the first regiment of foot-guards.

The poor man endeavoured to pacify his master by prayers and entreaties, but without success.—He then said to the officer, that there were some things in his room which he wished to put in order before he went, and desired that he might be allowed a little time for that purpose. The officer readily assented, and as soon as this desperate man had entered his own apartment, he seized a pistol, which he had prepared from the time the King had threatened him, and immediately shot himself through the head. The report of the pistol alarmed the King and the officer.—They both went into the room, and found the poor creature expiring.

Though the King certainly had no idea that his valet would shoot himself; and though, it is most probable, he would not have allowed him to remain long in the situation to which, in a fit of resentment, he had condemned him;—yet there is something exceedingly harsh in dashing a man at once from a situation of ease and respect, into a sphere of life so very different.— Such an order was more becoming the fury of an intemperate despot, than the dignity of so great and so wise a monarch as the King of Prussia.

I conversed with a person who had been at Sans-Souci immediately after this melancholy event.—He said the King seemed to be very much affected.—If he felt it as he ought, he was an object of compassion; if he did not, he was still more so, for nothing can be a greater misfortune to a man than to want humanity.

LETTER LXXIX.

Dresden.

I believe I neglected to mention in any of my letters from Berlin, that when I visited the manufactory of porcelain, I was so much struck with the beauty of some of it, that I ordered a small box for you. But as I take it to be a matter of indifference, whether you sip your tea out of the china you have already, or this, you may send it as a present to the female you love and esteem most. If by this direction it should not go straight from you to Miss ——, pray let me know to whom you send it. The factor at Hamburgh will give you notice when he ships it off.

I did not imagine that this manufactory had arrived at such a degree of perfection as it has in several places in Germany, particularly at Brunswic and Berlin. The parcel I have ordered for you, is thought equal to the finest made at Dresden.

The day we left Potsdam we dined with good Lord Marechal, who took leave of the D——, with an emotion which at once marked his regard for his G———, and his fears that he should never see him again.

If I were strongly in a humour for description, our journey through the most beautiful and most fertile part of Germany, would afford me a fair opportunity. I not only could ring over the whole chimes of woods, meadows, rivers, and mountains, rich crops of grain, flax, tobacco, and hops; I might animate the landscapes with a copious breed of horses, black cattle, sheep, wild boars, and venison, and vary the description with the marble, precious stones, and mines of lead, copper, iron, and silver, which Saxony contains within its bowels. I might expatiate on the fine china ware, and fine women, that abound in this country, formed of the finest clay in Germany, et très joliment travaillées;—but I am long since tired of description, and therefore beg leave to convey you at once from Potsdam to Dresden.

Having been presented to the Elector and Electress by Mr. Osborn, the British minister here, we had the honour of dining with them the same day. The Electress is young, tall, well-made, and lively.—We were afterwards presented to the Electress Dowager, and to the Princess Elizabeth, the Elector's aunt, to the Princess, his sister, and to his three brothers, the eldest of whom has lost the use of his legs, and is moved about the room in a chair with wheels.

The court was numerous and splendid. In the evening there was card-playing for about two hours. The D—— of H—— was of the Electress's party, while I played two rubbers at whist with one of the Princesses, against the

Electress Dowager and the Princess Elizabeth.—I have never seen deep gaming at any of the German courts.—What has approached nearest to it, has been at masquerades, or where the Sovereign was not present.

Dresden, though not one of the largest, is certainly one of the most agreeable cities in Germany, whether we consider its situation, the magnificence of its palaces, or the beauty and conveniency of the houses and streets. This city is built on both sides of the Elbe, which is of a considerable breadth here. The magnificent and commodious manner in which the two opposite parts of the town are joined, adds greatly to its beauty.

There is an equestrian statue of King Augustus, in a kind of open place or square, between the old city and the new. The workmanship is but indifferent; however, I was desired by our Cicerone to admire this very much, because—it was made by a common smith. I begged to be excused, telling him that I could not admire it, had it been made by Michael Angelo.

Few Princes in Europe are so magnificently lodged as the Elector of Saxony. The Palace and Museum have been often described.—The last was begun by the Elector Augustus, and still retains the name of the Green Room, though it now consists of several apartments, all painted green, in imitation of the first. I will not enumerate the prodigious number of curiosities, natural and artificial, to be seen there. Some of the last are curious, only because they are invisible to the human eye. Of this number, is a cherry stone, upon which, by the help of a microscope, above a hundred faces may be distinguished. Undoubtedly these little mechanical whims display the labour, perseverance, and minute attention of the workman; but I cannot think they are proofs of the wisdom of those who could employ artists to so little purpose. Let the astonishing minutiæ of nature be admired through microscopes; but surely nothing is a proper work for the hands of man, which cannot be seen by the unaided human eye.

A work of the jeweller Dinglinger, which represents the celebration of the Mogul's birth-day, is much admired. The Mogul sitting on his throne, his grandees and guards, with a great many elephants, are all exhibited upon a table about an ell square. This work employed Dinglinger, and some assistants, above ten years. Do not you think this was leaving so ingenious an artist a little too long in the Mogul's service?

A simple list of every thing valuable and curious in this Museum, would exceed the bounds of one of my longest letters; I shall therefore pass them all over in silence, except the story of the prophet Jonah, which it would be impious to omit. The ship, the whale, the prophet, and the sea-shore, are all represented in pearl; but the sea and rocks are in a different kind of stone, though, in my opinion, there was no occasion to vary the materials; for surely there is as great a difference between a prophet and a whale, as between a whale and a rock. So that if the first two could be represented with the same materials, I do not think it was worth while to change the composition for the third.

The gallery of pictures is highly esteemed. To enumerate the particular merits of each, would fill many volumes, and requires a far greater knowledge of painting than I can pretend to. The most valuable pieces are by Corregio and Rubens. There are three or four by the former, and of his most capital works; and a very considerable number by the latter. The strength and expression of this great artist's pencil, the natural glow of his colouring, and the fertility of his fancy deserve the highest encomiums. Yet one cannot help regretting, that he had so violent a passion for fat women. That kind of nature which he had seen early in life in his own country, had laid such hold of his imagination, that it could not be eradicated by all the elegant models he afterwards studied in Italy. Some of his female figures in this gallery are so much of the Dutch make, and so fat, that it is rather oppressive to look at them in this very hot weather.

In the Museum, within the Palace, there is a most complete collection of prints, from the commencement of the art of engraving till the present time.

LETTER LXXX.

Dresden.

Nothing seems clearer to me, than that a fortified town should have no palaces within it, and no suburbs without. As the city of Dresden has both, it would have been well for the inhabitants, during the last war, that the town had been entirely without fortifications. In the year 1756, when the King of Prussia thought it expedient to invade Saxony, he made himself master of this city, and kept peaceable possession of it till 1758, when Marechal Daun, after the battle of Hochkirchen, threatened to besiege it. The Prussian General Schmettau began his defence by burning part of the suburbs. The Saxons and Austrians exclaimed at this measure, and Daun threatened to make the governor answerable, in his own person, for such desperate proceedings. Count Schmettau was totally regardless of their exclamations and threats, and seemed attentive only to the orders of the King his master. He gave Marechal Daun to understand, that the remaining suburbs would share the fate of those already destroyed, if he persisted in attacking the town. The King appearing soon after, the Austrians retreated into Bohemia.

The inhabitants of Dresden, and all Saxony, were now in a very dismal situation, and found their hardships increase in proportion to the success of their friends and allies; for whatever exactions were raised in the King of Prussia's dominions by the Austrians and Russians, the like were imposed by way of retaliation on the miserable Saxons. A people must be in a deplorable state indeed, when the success of their enemies is the most fortunate thing which can befal them.

In 1759, after the dreadful battle of Cunersdorf, near Frankfort on the Oder, the King of Prussia being necessitated to repair the slaughter of that day, withdrew the Prussian garrison from Dresden, which then fell into the hands of the Imperialists. But the calamities of this city did not end here; for his Prussian Majesty having deceived Marechal Daun by a very masterly feint, while he seemed to bend his course for Silesia, he wheeled suddenly about, and threatened Dresden, which Marechal Daun had abandoned, in the full conviction, that the King had marched to the relief of Schweidnitz. While the Austrians hurried on by forced marches into Silesia, the King attacked Dresden, which was resolutely defended by General Macquire.

Every possible effort was made to reduce this city before Count Daun should return to its relief;—and the wretched citizens were exposed to a continued cannonade and bombardment. This perhaps was justifiable by the laws of war, as long as there were hopes that the town might be brought to surrender by such means.—But the enemies of his Prussian Majesty assert, that the bombardment was continued, and churches, fine buildings, and whole streets laid in ashes, even after Marechal Daun's return; and when these vindictive proceedings could only tend to the ruin and destruction of private people, without contributing in the smallest degree to the reducing the town, or being of any use to the public cause.

Many of these houses still lie in rubbish; but the inhabitants are gradually rebuilding, and probably all the ruined streets will be repaired before a new war breaks out in Germany. While they rebuild the houses, I cannot help thinking it would be fortunate for the proprietors, that they were allowed to destroy the fortifications, which perhaps might be placed with more advantage around some towns on the frontiers.

The curious manufactory of porcelain suffered considerably by the Prussian bombardment. The Elector has a complete collection of the finest pieces, from the first attempts made here in this elegant work, to the latest improvements. This, independent of the beauty of many of the pieces, is a matter of real curiosity, as it marks the progress of ingenuity and invention.

Our morning-walk is in the gardens of the late Count Bruhl, situated on the high banks of the Elbe. Nothing can be imagined more delightful than the view from a lofty terrace in these gardens. The Count's magnificent house is now stript of many of its greatest ornaments. The fine collection of paintings has been sold to the Empress of Russia for 150,000 rix-dollars. The library, which is in the garden, is two hundred and twenty feet long. I am not certain, whether it was absolutely necessary to have so large a room for containing this nobleman's books; but it must have required one of that size at least for his wardrobe, if the account that is given of it be just. They tell us, that the Count had at least three hundred different suits of clothes; each of these had a duplicate, as he always shifted his clothes after dinner, and did not choose that his dress should appear different in the afternoon from what it had been in the morning. A painting of each suit, with the particular cane and snuff-box belonging to it, was very accurately drawn in a large book, which was presented to his Excellency every morning by his Valet de Chambre, that he might fix upon the dress in which he wished to appear for the day. This minister was accused of having accumulated a great fortune. The reverse of this, however, is true. His house and gardens belong now to the Elector.

The Saxon troops make a very fine appearance. The men in general are handsome and well made. Neither they nor their officers are so very upright and stiff in their manners, as the Prussians. Having been so long accustomed to these last, this difference struck me very strongly at first sight. The uniform of the guards is red and yellow; that of the marching regiments white. The soldiers, during the summer, wear only waistcoats, even when they mount guard; and always appear extremely neat and clean. The serjeants, besides their other arms, have a large pistol. This is so commodiously fastened to the left side, that it gives no trouble. The band of music belonging to the Saxon guards is the most complete and the finest I ever saw.

I do not expect to receive any accounts from you till we arrive at Vienna; but I shall probably write again from Prague, for which place we intend to set out to-morrow.

LETTER LXXXI.

Bohemia, though by no means so fertile, or so fine a country as Saxony, does not deserve the bad character which some travellers have given it. I thought many places very beautiful, and varied with the most agreeable rural objects.

Prague, the capital of Bohemia, stands in a hollow, surrounded on all sides with hills. Those nearest the town, and which command it, are comprehended within the fortifications. It is a very large town, retaining some marks of former splendor, but many more evident symptoms of present decay—Symptoms which naturally attend those places which once have been the residence of royalty, and are so no more.

All the houses, with any appearance of magnificence, are old, and it is not probable, that any new ones will be built in that style: for the Bohemian nobility, who are in circumstances to bear such an expence, live at Vienna, and the trade and manufactures of this town are not sufficient to enable any of the mercantile people to build fine houses.

In whatever degree this city may have dwindled in wealth and magnificence, the piety of the inhabitants certainly flourishes as much as ever. I do not recollect to have seen so many glaring marks of devotion in any place. The corners of the streets, bridges, and public buildings, are all ornamented with crucifixes, images of the Virgin of all sizes and complexions, and statues of Saints of every country, condition, age, and sex. People are to be seen on their knees before these statues in every part of this city, but particularly on the large bridge over the Moldaw, where there is the greatest concourse of passengers. This bridge is so profusely adorned with the statues of Saints, that crossing over it, you have a row of them on each side, like two ranks of musketeers.

Travellers, especially such as arrive directly from Berlin, must be astonished at the people's devotion in this city, in a particular manner at the vehemence with which it is expressed by those who exhibit before the saints upon the bridge.

Not contented with kneeling, I saw some prostrate themselves on their faces, kissing the earth; and others, who offered their petitions to these saints with such earnestness and fervour, that, if their hearts had not been of stone, they must have paid more attention to the petitioners than they seemed to do.

There is one saint who has more votaries than all the rest put together—Saint Nepomuc, I think they call him:—As my acquaintance with saints is not extensive, I never heard of him till I came hither, but his reputation is very great in this town. This saint, it seems, was ordered by some cruel tyrant, to be thrown over a bridge, and his neck was broke by the fall, and he is supposed to retain a particular affection for bridges ever since; an effect something different from what was to have been expected from the cause; however, the people here are persuaded, that so it happened to Saint Nepomuc; and to put the fact beyond controversy, he is at this moment the tutelar saint of bridges;—almost all those in Bohemia are dedicated to him. He has also the reputation of excelling every saint in heaven in the cure of barrenness in women.—How his character for this was established, I did not enquire.

It is a melancholy reflection, that the wealthy are more careless about religious duties than the indigent, and that poverty and piety are so often linked together. I often observed, when we stopped at any town or village, which had symptoms of great poverty, that the inhabitants seemed also unusually devout.

It would appear, that hope is a more powerful sentiment in the human breast than gratitude, since those who ought to feel the greatest thankfulness to Heaven display the least.

We found an acquaintance at Prague when we least expected it; for as the D—— of H—— and I stood talking in the streets, a priest, who belongs to a seminary of learning in this town, overheard us; upon which he stopped, and after looking at us very earnestly for some time, he at length came up, and addressed us in these words:—I do assure you now, I am an Irishman too. This easy kind of introduction soon produced a degree of intimacy; I asked how he knew so readily that we were Irish? Am I not after hearing you speak English, my dear? replied the honest priest, for he really was a very honest obliging fellow, and the most useful and entertaining Cicerone we could have had at Prague.

After having visited the royal apartments, they shewed us the window in the secretary of state's office, from whence three noblemen were thrown in the year 1618. This was rather a violent mode of turning out the people in power; but it is probable the party in opposition had tried gentler means in vain.

As one great use of history is to furnish lessons and examples, by which posterity in all ages may profit, I do not think it would be amiss to remind your friends in administration of this adventure, that they may move off quietly before their opponents take desperate measures. For it has been observed, that the enemies of tottering statesmen are much more active than their friends, who, when things come to the last push, are apt to stand aloof,

Like people viewing, at a distance,

Three men thrown out of a casement,

Who never stir to their assistance,

But just afford them their amazement.

In case however a similar outrage should be threatened in England, it is to be hoped that Apollo (as he was wont of old when any of his friends were in danger) will interpose with a cloud, and save the Minister; for, in the present scarcity of wit and good humour, it would be a thousand pities to lose a man so much distinguished for both, at one desperate throw.

We walked over the heights from which the Prussians attempted to carry the town, immediately after the defeat of Prince Charles of Lorraine and Count Brown. The bombardment of this town was a more defensible measure than that of Dresden; for while the army within were under the dejection natural after the loss of a battle, and unprepared for a siege, it might be supposed, that the confusion and terror produced by the bombardment, joined to the vast consumption of provisions by such a numerous garrison, would induce the besieged to surrender. But although the King's humanity has not been called in question for his conduct here, I have heard many military men censure him for want of prudence, particularly on account of his desperate attempt at Kolin, when, leaving the half of his army to continue the blockade of Prague, he marched with little more than thirty thousand men, and attacked an army of double that number, strongly situated, and commanded by one of the ablest generals of the age.

After all, it is more than probable, that the King had very good reasons for his conduct. But as the attempt was unsuccessful, and as the sad reverse of the Prussian affairs may be dated from that epoch, the voice of censure has been very loud in blaming an action, which would have been exalted to the skies had it been crowned with success. If Hannibal had by any accident been defeated at Cannæ, it is very possible, that historians would have found out many reasons why he should not have fought that battle, and would have endeavoured to prove, that his former victories had been gained by chance, and that he was a mere ignoramus in the art of war.

Adieu, my good friend; I wish you good luck in all your undertakings, that you may continue to be reckoned by the world, a man of prudence.

LETTER LXXXII.

Vienna.

On arriving at Vienna, the postillions drive directly to the Custom-house, where the baggage undergoes a very severe scrutiny, which neither fair words nor money can mitigate. As nothing contraband was found among our baggage, it was all carried directly to our lodgings, except our books, which were retained to be examined at leisure, and were not restored to us till some time after. The Empress has given strict orders, that no books of impiety, lewdness, or immorality, shall be allowed to enter her dominions, or be circulated among her subject; and Mahomet himself dares as soon appear publicly at Vienna as any one of them.

Unfortunately for us, Sir Robert Keith is lately gone to England, and is not expected back for several months. We have reason to regret the absence of so agreeable and so worthy a man; but every advantage we could have received from him as a minister, has been supplied by his secretary, Mr. Ernest, who has introduced us to the Count Degenfelt, ambassador from the States-General. This gentleman furnished us with a list of the visits proper to be made, and had the politeness to attend the D—— of H—— on this grand tour.

The first day we waited on Prince Kaunitz, we were invited to dine, and found a very numerous company at his house, many of whom, as I afterwards understood, had been prepossessed in our favour, by the polite and obliging letters which the Baron de Swieten had written from Berlin.

Some of the principal families are at their seats in the country, which we should have more reason to regret, were it not for the politeness and hospitality of the Count and Countess Thune, at whose house, or that of their sister the Countess Walstein, there is an agreeable party every evening; among whom is the Viscount de Laval, brother to the Marquis, whom I had the honour of knowing at Berlin. The Viscount has been as far north as Petersburg, and intends to make the tour of Italy before he returns to France.

The city of Vienna, properly so called, is not of very great extent; nor can it be enlarged, being limited by a strong fortification. This town is very populous: It is thought to contain above seventy thousand inhabitants. The streets in general are narrow, and the houses built high. Some of the public buildings and palaces are magnificent; but they appear externally to no great advantage, on account of the narrowness of the streets. The chief are the Imperial Palace, the Library and Museum, the palaces of the Princes

Lichtenstein, Eugene, and some others, which I know you will excuse me from enumerating or describing.

There is no great danger that Vienna will ever again be subjected to the inconveniencies of a siege. Yet, in case the thing should happen, a measure has been taken, which will prevent the necessity of destroying the suburbs: No houses without the walls are allowed to be built nearer to the glacis than six hundred yards; so that there is a circular field of six hundred paces broad all around the town, which, exclusive of the advantage above mentioned, has a very beautiful and salutary effect. Beyond the plain, the suburbs are built.— They form a very extensive and magnificent town of an irregularly circular form, containing within its bosom a spacious field, which has for its centre the original town of Vienna.

These magnificent suburbs, and the town together, are said to contain above three hundred thousand inhabitants; yet the former are not near so populous, in proportion to their size, as the town; because many houses of the suburbs have extensive gardens belonging to them, and many families, who live during the winter within the fortifications, pass the summer months in the suburbs.

Monsieur de Breteuil, the French ambassador, lives there at present. The Duke and I dined at his house a few days ago. This gentleman was attached to the Duc de Choiseul, and had been appointed ambassador to this court, in which character he was about to set out from Paris, when that minister was dismissed by the late King of France; upon which M. de Breteuil, instead of Vienna, was sent to Naples. But since the new King's accession, he has been established at the court for which he was originally intended. He is a man of talents, and not calculated for a situation in which talents have little or no room for exertion.

About a week after our arrival at Vienna, we had the honour of being presented to the Emperor. The Count Degenfeldt accompanied us to the palace between nine and ten in the morning. After walking a few minutes in an adjoining room, we were conducted into that where the Emperor was alone. His manner is affable, easy, and gracefully plain.

The same forenoon we drove to Schonbrun, a palace about a league from Vienna, where the Empress resides at present. I had no small curiosity to see the celebrated Maria Theresa, whose fortunes have interested Europe for so many years. Her magnanimity in supporting the calamities to which the early part of her life was exposed, and the moderation with which she has borne prosperity, have secured to her universal approbation. She also was alone when we were presented. She conversed for some time with the D——— of

H—— in an easy and cheerful manner, and behaved to all with an affable dignity. She now possesses but small remains of that beauty for which she was distinguished in her youth; but her countenance indicates benevolence and good-humour. I had often heard of the scrupulous etiquette of the Imperial court, but have found every thing directly opposite to that account.

Prince Kaunitz having seen a young English gentleman scarcely fourteen years of age, whom the D—— of H—— patronizes, and who has accompanied us on this tour, the Prince desired that he also might be presented to the Emperor and Empress, which was accordingly done, and they both received him in the most gracious manner. I mention this circumstance as a strong proof how far they are superior at this court to trifling punctilios, and how greatly they have relaxed in ceremony since the accession of the Lorrain family.

Two or three days after this, we were presented, at a full court, to the two unmarried Arch-Duchesses, their sister the Princess Albert of Saxony, and the Princess of Modena, who is married to the Emperor's brother. The last couple are lately arrived from Milan on a visit to the Empress.

The Imperial family are uncommonly well-looking, and have a very strong resemblance to each other. They are all of a fair complexion, with large blue eyes, and some of them, particularly the Arch-duke, are distinguished by the thick lip so long remarked in the Austrian family. The beautiful Queen of France is the handsomest of this family, only because she is the youngest; some people think that her sister the Princess Albert has still the advantage.

One of the unmarried Arch-duchesses, who formerly was thought the most beautiful, has suffered considerably by the small-pox.—A lady of the court told me, that, as soon as this princess understood what her disease was, she called for a looking-glass, and with unaffected pleasantry took leave of those features she had often heard praised, and which she believed would be greatly changed before she should see them again. The diminution which the small-pox has made in the beauty of this Princess, has not in the smallest degree impaired her good-humour, or the essential part of her character, which by every account is perfectly amiable.

When the King of Prussia saw his army defeated at Cunersdorf, after he had written to the Queen that he was sure of victory; or when any of those monarchs, of whom history gives examples, were dashed from their thrones to a state of dependence or captivity, unquestionably it required great strength of mind to bear such cruel reverses of fortune; but perhaps it requires more in a woman, whose beauty is admired by one half of the human race, and envied by the other, to support its loss with equanimity in all the pride of youth.—If those veteran beauties, who never had any thing but their faces to give them importance, whom we see still withering on the stalk, and repining that they cannot retain the bloom of May in the frost of December, had met with such an accident, it would probably have killed them at once, and saved them many years of despised existence.

LETTER LXXXIII.

Vienna.

I never passed my time more agreeably than since I came to Vienna. There is not such a constant round of amusements as to fill up a man's time without any plan or occupation of his own; and yet there is enough to satisfy any mind not perfectly vacant and dependent on external objects.—We dine abroad two or three times a week. We sometimes see a little play, but never any deep gaming.—At the Countess Thune's, where I generally pass the evening, there is no play of any kind.—The society there literally form a conversazione.

I dare say, you will be at a loss to imagine how a mixed company, sometimes pretty numerous, can pass several hours every evening, merely in conversing, especially when you are told that the conversation is not always split into parties and tête-à-têtes; but is very often general. You will suspect there must be many melancholy pauses, which, after a certain length, are prolonged, from the reluctance of people to be the first breakers of a very solemn silence; or you may think that sometimes there will be so many tongues moving at once, that nothing can be heard distinctly; and you may possibly figure to yourself the lady of the house at other times endeavouring, by formal observations on the weather, or politics, to keep alive a conversation which is just expiring in all the yawnings of death.

Nothing of this kind, however, happens. The Countess has the art of entertaining a company, and of making them entertain one another, more than any person I ever knew. With a great deal of wit, and a perfect knowledge of the world, she possesses the most disinterested heart. She is the first to discover the good qualities of her friends, and the last who sees their foibles. One of her greatest pleasures is to remove prejudices from amongst her acquaintances, and to promote friendships. She has an everlasting flow of spirits, which she manages with such address as to delight the gay, without displeasing the dejected. I never knew any body have such a number of friends, and so much generous friendship to bestow on each: She is daily making new ones, without allowing her regard for the old to diminish. She has formed a little system of happiness at her own house, herself being the centre of attraction and union. Nobody is under the least necessity of remaining a moment in this society after being tired.—They may retire when they please.—No more notice is taken of the entries or exits of any person who has been once received, than of a fly's coming in or going out of the room.—There is not the shadow of restraint.—If you go every night, you are always treated with equal kindness; and if you stay away for a month, you are received on your return with the same cheerfulness as if you had been there every evening.

The English who come to this place are in a particular manner obliged to this family, not only for the polite reception they generally meet with, but also for the opportunities this affords them of forming an acquaintance with the principal people at Vienna. And I imagine there is no city in Europe where a young gentleman, after his university education is finished, can pass a year with so great advantage; because, if properly recommended, he may mix, on an easy footing, with people of rank, and have opportunities of improving by the conversation of sensible men and accomplished women. In no capital could he see fewer examples, or have fewer opportunities of deep gaming, open profligacy, or gross debauchery. He may learn to pass his time agreeably, independent of a continued round of amusements.—He may be gradually led to enjoy rational conversation, and at length acquire the blessed faculty of being satisfied with moderate pleasures.

To the politeness of the Countess Thune, and the recommendation of the Baron Swieten, I am indebted for the agreeable footing I am on with Prince Kaunitz, who at present lives at Laxenberg, a pleasant village about ten miles from Vienna, where there is a small palace and very extensive park, belonging to the Imperial family.

Prince Kaunitz has lately built a house there, and lives in a style equally hospitable and magnificent. He is not to be seen before dinner by any but people on business; but he always has a pretty large company at dinner, and still greater numbers from Vienna pass their evenings at Laxenberg; not unfrequently the Emperor himself makes one of the company. This minister has enjoyed the favour of the Empress for many years. He was her envoy at the treaty of Aix la Chapelle in 1748, and has been of her cabinet council ever since. At present he is minister for all foreign affairs, and is supposed to have greater influence with her than any other person.

He is certainly a man of knowledge, genius, and fidelity, and the affairs of this court have prospered greatly under his management. His friends are very much attached to him, and he shews great discernment in discovering, and employing men of talents. He is the friend and patron of Mons. de Swieten. It is supposed that he advised and negociated the French alliance, yet he has always had a strong partiality in favour of the British nation.—He has some singularities; but as they do not affect any essential part of his character, they need not be mentioned.

LETTER LXXXIV.

Vienna.

I had the pleasure of yours by the last post, wherein you inform me that our acquaintance C—— talks of setting out for Vienna very soon. As nothing is so tiresome as the company of one who is continually tired of himself, I should be alarmed at your information, were I not absolutely certain that his stay here will be very short, come when he will.

C—— called at my lodgings one morning the summer before I had left London.—I had remained in town merely because I had no particular business elsewhere;—but he assured me, that the town was a desert;—that it was shameful to be seen in the streets;—that all the world was a Brighthelmstone.—So I allowed him to conduct me to that place, where we had remained only a few days, when he told me, that none of the people he cared for were there; and as I had nothing particular to detain me, he begged as a favour that I would accompany him to Tunbridge.—We went accordingly, and to my great satisfaction I there found Mr. N——'s family. C—— remained pretty quiet for about four days;—he yawned a good deal on the fifth;—and on the sixth, I thought he would have dislocated his jaws. As he perceived I was pleased with the place, and would take none of his hints about leaving it, he at last pretended that he had received a letter which made it absolutely necessary for him to set out for London:—and away he went.

I staid three weeks at Tunbridge.—On my return to town, I understood that C—— had taken a genteel furnished house for the summer, in Yorkshire, where he had already passed a week, having previously engaged a female friend to go along with him.—He left word in town, that he was not to be expected till the meeting of parliament. Though I never imagined that he would remain quite so long, yet I was a little surprised to see him enter my room two days after I had received this account.—He told me, he was quite disgusted with his house, and more so with his companion:—and besides, he had taken a violent fancy to go to Paris, which you know, added he, is the most delightful place in the world, especially in summer; for the company never think of rambling about the country like our giddy fools in England, but remain together in the capital as sensible people ought to do.

He then proposed that we should pack up a few things,—take post,—pass over,—and spend a couple of months at Paris. Finding I did not relish the proposal, he wrote an apology to the lady in Yorkshire, with an inclosed bank bill, and set out next day by himself. I heard no more of him for six weeks, but at the end of that time happening to be at Bath, I saw my friend C—— enter the pump-room.—'Egad, said he, you were wise to stay at home:—

Paris is become the most insipid place on earth:—I could not support it above ten days.—But having heard a good deal of Holland, I even took a jaunt to Amsterdam, which, between friends, I found very little more amusing than Paris; two days after my arrival, finding an English ship just ready to sail, I thought it would be a pity to let the opportunity slip. So I ordered my trunk aboard.—We had a disagreeable passage:—However, I arrived safe a few days ago at Harwich. After this sketch of poor C——'s turn of mind, you see, I have no reason to fear his remaining long with us, if he should come.

Foreigners assert that the English have more of this restless disposition than any other people in Europe.

Il faut que votre ville de Londres soit un triste séjour.—I asked the person who made this remark to me, wherefore he thought so?—Parceque, answered he, tous vos jeunes gens que je vois en France s'ennuyent à la mort.—But, said I, there are a great many of your countrymen in London.— Assurément, answered he, with polite insolence, cela fait une différence.

Our climate is accused of producing this ennuy. If I rightly remember, I formerly hinted some reasons against this opinion, and of late I begin to suspect that the excessive wealth of certain individuals, and the state of society in our capital, are the sole causes of our having a greater share of that malady among us than our neighbours. The common people of England know nothing of it:—neither do the industrious of any rank, whether their object be wealth, knowledge, or fame. But in England there is a greater number than in any other country, of young men, who come to the possession of great fortunes before they have acquired any fixed and determined taste, which may serve as a resource and occupation through life.

When a youth has acquired a habit of application, a thirst of knowledge, or of fame, the most ample fortune which can fall to him afterwards, cannot always destroy dispositions and passions already formed—Particularly if the passion be ambition, which generally gives such energy to the mind, and occasions such continued exertions as sufficiently ward off lassitude and tædium; for wealth cannot lull, or pleasure enervate, a mind strongly inspired by that active principle. Such therefore are out of the present question. But when a full and uncontrolled command of money comes first, and every object of pleasure is placed within the reach of the unambitious, all other pursuits are too frequently despised; and every taste or accomplishment which could inform or strengthen the mind, and fill up the tedious intervals of life, is neglected.

A young man in this situation is prone to excess, he seldom waits the natural returns of appetite of any kind;—his sensibility is blunted by too frequent enjoyment;—what is desired to-day, is lothed to-morrow;—every thing at a distance, which bears the name of pleasure, is an object of desire;—when present, it becomes an object of indifference, if not of disgust.—The agitations of gaming are tried to prevent the horrid stagnation of indolence:—All amusements lose their relish, and serve to increase the languor they were meant to expel.

As age advances, caprice, peevishness, and tædium augment:—The scene is often changed; but the same fretful piece is constantly acted till the curtain is dropt, or is pulled down by the impatient actor himself before the natural end of the drama.

Does not all this happen in France and Germany?—Doubtless; but not so often as in England, for the reasons already mentioned. In France, a very small proportion of young men have the uncontrolled possession of great fortunes. They have not the means of gratifying every desire, and indulging every caprice. Instead of spending their time in clubs or taverns, with people of their own age, the greater part of the young nobility pass their evenings with some private family, or in those societies of both sexes to which they have the entrée. There the decorum due to such company restrains of course the vivacity and wantonness of their behaviour and conversation; and adventures occur which interest and amuse, without being followed by the nausea, languor, and remorse, which often succeed nights spent at the gaming-table, or the licentiousness of tavern suppers.

Nothing has a better influence on the temper, disposition, and manners of a young person, than living much in the company of those whom he respects. Exclusive of the improvement he may receive from their conversation, he is habituated to self-denial, and must relinquish many indulgencies which lead to indolence and languor.

The young French nobility, even although they should have no great share of ambition, no love of study, no particular turn for any of those higher accomplishments which enable men to pass the hours of life independent of other amusements; yet they contrive to keep tædium at a distance by efforts of a different kind, by a species of activity peculiar to themselves; they perceive very early in life, the absolute necessity of pleasing. This sentiment pervades their general conduct, and goes a great way in the formation of their real character. They are attentive and obliging to all, and particularly endeavour to acquire and retain the friendship of those who can assist their fortunes; and they have a relish for life, because it is not always in their power to anticipate enjoyment, nor can they cloy their appetites by satiety. Even the most dissipated among them are unacquainted with the unbounded freedom of a tavern life, where all the freaks of a whimsical mind, and a capricious taste, may be indulged without hesitation, and which, after long indulgence, renders every other kind of society insupportable.

With regard to the Germans, there are very few men of great independent fortunes among them. The little princes, by whom the riches of the country are engrossed, have, I suspect, their own difficulties to get through life with any tolerable degree of satisfaction. As for their younger brothers and the middling gentry, they go into the army, and are subjected to the rigorous and unremitting attentions of military discipline. This, of consequence, forms a character, in many respects different from that of the English or French gentleman.

But I have not yet mentioned the circumstance, which, of all others, perhaps contributes the most to render London the triste séjour which foreigners often find it; I mean the establishment of clubs, from which that part of the community are excluded who have the greatest power to soothe the cares, and enliven the pleasures of life.

LETTER LXXXV.

Vienna.

We had an invitation lately from Mons. de Breteuil to dine on the top of Mount Calenberg, a very high mountain in the neighbourhood of this city. Common coaches or chariots cannot be dragged up; but having driven to the bottom, we found chaises of a particular construction, calculated for such expeditions. These had been ordered by the Ambassador for the accommodation of the company, and in them we were carried to the summit, where there is a convent of Monks, from which two landscapes of very opposite natures appear. The one consists of a series of wild mountains; the other, of the town, suburbs, and environs of Vienna, with the various branches of the Danube flowing through a rich champaign of boundless extent.

The table for dinner was covered in a field near the convent, under the shade of some trees.—Every delicacy of the season was served up.—— Madame de Matignon, a very beautiful and sprightly lady, daughter of M. de Breteuil, did the honours.—Some of the finest women of Vienna, her companions, were of the company; and the whole entertainment was conducted with equal taste and gaiety.

During the dessert, some of the Fathers came and presented the company with baskets of fruit and sallad from their garden.—The Ambassador invited them to sit, and the ladies pledged them in tokay. Mons. de Breteuil had previously obtained permission for the ladies to enter the convent;—— which they accordingly did, as soon as they rose from table, attended by all the company.

You will readily believe, that the appearance of so many handsome women would be particularly interesting to a community which had never before beheld a female within their walls.—This indeed was sufficiently evident, in spite of the gravity and mortified looks of the Fathers.

One lady of a gay disposition laid hold of a little scourge which hung at one of the Fathers' belts, and desired he would make her a present of it, for she wished to use it when she returned home, having, as she said, been a great sinner.—— The Father, with great gallantry, begged she would spare her own fair skin, assuring her that he would give himself a hearty flogging on her account that very evening;—and to prove how much he was in earnest, fell directly on his knees before a little altar, and began to whip his own shoulders with great earnestness, declaring, that when the ladies should retire, he would lay it with the same violence on his naked body; for he was determined she should be as free from sin as she was on the day of her birth.

This melted the heart of the lady.—She begged the Father might take no more of her faults upon his shoulders.——— She now assured him that her slips had been very venial, and that she was convinced what he had already done would clear her as completely as if he should whip himself to the bone.

There is something so ludicrous in all this, that you may naturally suspect the representation I have given, proceeds from invention rather than memory. I assure you, however, in downright earnest, that the scene passed nearly as described; and to prevent farther mischief, I put the scourge, which the zealous Father had made use of, in my pocket.

On my return to Vienna, I called the same evening at the Countess Walstein's, and soon after the Emperor came there. Somebody had already mentioned to him the pious gallantry of the Father at the top of Mount Calenberg.—He asked for a sight of the whip, which he understood I had brought away:—I had it still in my pocket, and immediately showed it him.—— He laughed very heartily at the warmth of the Father's zeal, which he supposed had been augmented by the Ambassador's tokay.

You have often heard of the unceremonious and easy manner in which this great Prince lives with his subjects. Report cannot exaggerate on this head. The Countess Walstein had no expectations of his visiting her that evening.——— When the servant named the Emperor before he entered, I started up, and was going to retire.—The Countess desired me to remain, for nothing was more disagreeable to him than that any company should be disturbed on his entering.—The ladies kept their seats, some of them knotting all the time he remained. The men continued standing while he stood, and when he was seated, most part of them sat down also.—The Emperor put Count Mahoni, the Spanish ambassador, in mind of his gout, and made him sit, while himself remained standing.

This monarch converses with all the ease and affability of a private gentleman, and gradually seduces others to talk with the same ease to him. He is surely much happier in this noble condescension, and must acquire a more perfect knowledge of mankind, than if he kept himself aloof from his subjects, continually wrapt up in his own importance and the Imperial fur.

LETTER LXXXVI.

Vienna.

The manners of this court are considerably altered since Lady Mary Wortley Montague was here, particularly since the accession of the present Empress, whose understanding and affability have abridged many of the irksome ceremonials formerly in use. Her son's philosophical turn of mind, and the amiable and conciliating characters of her whole family, have no doubt tended to put society in general upon a more easy and agreeable footing.

People of different ranks now do business together with ease, and meet at public places without any of those ridiculous disputes about precedency, of which the ingenious English lady has given such lively descriptions.—Yet trifling punctilios are not so completely banished, as I imagine, the Emperor could wish, he himself being the least punctilious person in his dominions:—for there is certainly still a greater separation than good sense would direct, between the various classes of the subjects.—The sentiments of a people change very gradually, and it takes a course of years before reason, or even the example of the Sovereign, can overcome old customs and prejudices.

The higher, or ancient families, keep themselves as distinct from the inferior, or newly-created nobility, as these do from the citizens: So that it is very difficult for the inferior classes to be in society, or to have their families much connected with those of the superior ranks. And what is of more importance in a political sense, there are certain places of high trust in the government, which cannot be occupied by any but the higher order of nobility.

Would you not think it disadvantageous for a government to keep a law in force which enacts, that the offices in the state which require the greatest abilities, should be filled from that class of the community in which there is the least chance of finding them?—Perhaps the usage above mentioned is nearly equivalent to such a law. As for the peasants, who are entirely out of the question, they are, in many parts of the Emperor's dominions, in a state of perfect slavery, and almost totally dependent on the proprietors of the land.

The ideas relative to dress seem to have entirely changed since Lady Mary's time, and if the dress of the ladies be still as absurd, it is at least not so singular; for they, like the rest of Europe, have now adopted the Parisian modes.

The present race of Austrian ladies can differ in nothing more than they do in looks from their grandmothers, who, if any of them were still alive, may be as beautiful at this day as they were when she wrote; for time itself could hardly improve that ugliness, which, according to her, was in full bloom sixty years ago. I have not as yet enquired what method the parents have devised to remedy this inconveniency; but nothing is more certain than that it is remedied very effectually, for at present there is no scarcity of female beauty at the court of Vienna.

This being the case, it is natural to imagine that gallantry must now be more prevalent than when her ladyship was here. But exclusive of any real difference, which may have happened in the sentiments of the ladies themselves, they are obliged to observe an uncommon degree of circumspection in that particular, as nothing is more heinous in the eyes of her Imperial Apostolic Majesty. She seems to think that the ladies of her court, like the wife of Cæsar, should not only be free from guilt, but, what is still more difficult, free from suspicion, and strongly marks by her manner, that she is but too well informed when any piece of scandal circulates to the prejudice of any of them.

With regard to what Lady Mary calls sub-marriages, and of which she has given such a curious account, I do not imagine they are common at present, in all the latitude of her description. But it is not uncommon for married ladies here to avow the greatest degree of friendship and attachment to men who are not their husbands, and to live with them in great intimacy, without hurting their reputation, or being suspected, even by their own sex, of having deviated from the laws of modesty.

One evening at the Count Thune's, when there was a pretty numerous company, I observed one lady uncommonly sad, and enquired of her intimate friend who happened to be there also, if she knew the cause of this sadness?—I do, replied she; Mr. de ——, whom she loves very tenderly, ought to have been here a month ago; and last night she received a letter from him, informing her that he cannot be at Vienna for a month to come. But pray, said I, does your friend's husband know of this violent passion she has for Mr. de ——? Yes, yes, answered she, he knows it, and enters with the most tender sympathy into her affliction; he does all that can be expected from an affectionate husband to comfort and soothe his wife, assuring her that her love will wear away with time. But she always declares that she has no hopes of this, because she feels it augment every day.—Mais, au fond, continued the lady, cela lui fait bien de la peine, parceque malheureusement il aime sa femme à la folie. Et sa femme, qui est la meilleure créature du monde, plaint infiniment son pauvre mari; car elle a beaucoup d'amitié et d'estime pour lui;—mais elle ne scauroit se défaire de cette malheureuse passion pour Mons. de ——.

I was not in the least surprised that a disappointment of this nature should affect a woman a little; but I own it did astonish me that she should appear in public, on such an occasion, in all the ostentation of sorrow, like a young widow vain of her weeds. Here this passion was lamented by her friends as a misfortune: In England, if I rightly remember, such misfortunes are generally imputed to people as crimes.

LETTER LXXXVII.

The Viscount de Laval having proposed to me lately to make a short tour with him into Hungary, I very readily consented, and we arrived at this town yesterday morning.

Presburg, which is the capital of Lower Hungary, like Vienna, has suburbs more magnificent than itself. In this city the States of Hungary hold their assemblies, and in the cathedral church the Sovereign is crowned.

The present Empress took refuge here when the Elector of Bavaria was declared Emperor at Prague, when she was abandoned by her allies, and when France had planned her destruction. Her own magnanimity, the generous friendship of Great Britain, and the courage of her Hungarian subjects, at length restored her fortunes, and secured to her family the splendid situation they now hold in Europe.

What politician in 1741 could have thought that in the course of a few years the Empress would be in strict alliance with France, and one of her daughters seated on the throne of that kingdom?—Should a soothsayer of Boston prophesy, that John Hancock, or his son, will, sometime hence, demand in marriage a daughter of England,—pray, do not lay an uncommon odds, that the thing will not happen.

Mons. de Laval and I walked up this morning to the castle, which is a noble Gothic building, of a square form, with a tower at each corner. The regalia of Hungary, consisting of the crown and sceptre of St. Stephen, the first king, are deposited here. These are carefully secured by seven locks, the keys of which are kept by the same number of Hungarian noblemen. No Prince is held by the populace as legally their Sovereign till he be crowned with the diadem of King Stephen; and they have a notion that the fate of their nation depends on this crown's remaining in their possession. It has therefore been always removed in times of danger to places of the greatest safety.

The Turks, aware of the influence of such a prejudice in the minds of the vulgar, have, it is said, made frequent attempts to seize this Palladium.—The fate of Hungary seems now to be pretty much decided; so that exclusive of the value they put upon the crown, as a relic of considerable antiquity, the Hungarians need not be solicitous whether it remains in this castle or in the Imperial palace at Vienna.

By the constitution of Hungary, the crown is still held to be elective. This point is not disputed. All that is insisted on is, that the heir of the House of Austria shall be elected as often as a vacancy happens.

The castle of Presburg is the usual residence of Prince Albert of Saxony, who married one of the Arch-duchesses, a very beautiful and accomplished Princess. As M. de Laval and I entered one of the rooms, we observed them at a window. We immediately started back, and withdrew, being in riding frocks and boots. Mons. de Laval had seen their Highnesses a few days before at Schonbrun, and thought they had been there still. The Princess sent a polite message after us by a servant, who had orders to conduct us through every apartment of the castle; she herself stept into another room, that we might see that which she left.

All the Princesses of the Austrian family are distinguished by an attentive and obliging politeness, which is the more remarkable, as those who live much at courts often acquire a species of politeness which is by no means obliging. The splendor and distinctions of a court frequently inspire an overweening vanity, and have a peculiar tendency to shake the steadiness of the female understanding. Court ladies in general, but particularly such as submit to be abject sycophants to Queens and Princesses, are apt to render themselves ridiculous by the arrogant airs they assume to the rest of the world, and while they usurp the importance of royalty, fill the breasts of all who know them with as much detestation as is consistent with contempt.

The view from this citadel is very extensive, commanding the vast and fertile plains of Hungary.

Having dined at the inn, and regaled ourselves, at no great expence, with tokay, we went to visit a villa at the distance of four miles from Presburg, belonging to a Hungarian nobleman. This house is delightfully situated,— the gardens laid out a little too methodically; but the park, and fields around, where less art has been used, display a vast luxuriancy of natural beauties.— While wandering over these, we entered a little wood in a very retired place; as we advanced into this, we saw a venerable looking old man with a long beard, who, stretching out his hand, seemed to invite us to an hermitage which we observed hard by.

The Viscount, impatient to cultivate the acquaintance of a person of such an hospitable appearance, ran before me toward him; when he got up to him, he stopped short, as if surprised, and then, to my utter astonishment, he raised his foot with every mark of indignation, and gave the poor old hermit a violent kick.

I do not remember that I was ever more shocked in my life; I was at the same time quite confounded at an action so unworthy in itself, and so incompatible with the character of Mons. de Laval.—I was soon reconciled, however, to the treatment the old fellow had received, when I discovered that this venerable personage was not the honest man we took him for, but a downright impostor, made of painted wood, and dressed in the robes of a hermit to deceive passengers.

Over the door was an inscription from Horace—

Odi profanum vulgus,

On the inside of the door—

Fata volentes ducunt, nolentes trahunt.

And in another part, within the hermitage—

Omnes eodem cogimur: omnium

Versatur urna, serius ocius,

Sors exitura, et nos in æternum

Exilium impositura Cymbæ.

There were also several inscriptions taken from Cicero, in favour of the soul's immortality, which I am sorry I neglected to transcribe.—We returned in the evening to this place, and are to set out to-morrow for Prince Estherhasie's.

LETTER LXXXVIII.

Having left Presburg, we travelled eight posts across a very fertile country to the palace of Estherhasie, the residence of the Prince of that name. He is the first in rank of the Hungarian nobility, and one of the most magnificent subjects in Europe. He has body-guards of his own, all genteel-looking men, richly dressed in the Hungarian manner.

The palace is a noble building, lately finished, and situated near a fine lake. The apartments are equally grand and commodious: the furniture more splendid than almost any thing I have seen in royal palaces. In the Prince's own apartment there are some curious musical clocks, and one in the shape of a bird, which whistles a tune every hour.

Just by the palace, there is a theatre for operas, and other dramatic entertainments, and in the gardens, a large room with commodious apartments for masquerades and balls.

At no great distance, there is another theatre expressly built for puppet-shows. This is much larger and more commodious than most provincial playhouses, and I am bold to assert, is the most splendid that has as yet been reared in Europe for that species of actors. We regretted that we could not have the pleasure of seeing them perform; for they have the reputation of being the best comedians in Hungary.

We had the curiosity to peep behind the curtain, and saw Kings, Emperors, Turks, and Christians, all ranged very sociably together.—King Solomon was observed in a corner in a very suspicious tête-à-tête with the Queen of Sheba.

Amongst other curiosities, there is in the garden a wooden house, built upon wheels. It contains a room with a table, chairs, a looking-glass, chimney, and fire-place. There are also closets, with many necessary accommodations.— The Prince sometimes entertains twelve people in this vehicle, all of whom may easily sit round the table, and the whole company may thus take an airing together along the walks of the garden, and many parts of the park, which are as level as a bowling-green. The machine, when thus loaded, is easily drawn by six or eight horses.

Prince Estherhasie having heard of M. de Laval's being in the garden, sent us an invitation to the opera, which was to be performed that evening; but as we had brought with us no dress proper for such an occasion, we were forced to decline this obliging invitation.—The Prince afterwards sent a carriage, in which we drove round the garden and parks. These are of vast extent, and beautiful beyond description; arbours, fountains, walks, woods, hills, and valleys, being thrown together in a charming confusion.—If you will look over Ariosto's description of the gardens in Alcina's inchanted island, you will have an idea of the romantic fields of Estherhasie, which are also inhabited by the same kind of animals.

Tra le purpuree rose e i bianchi gigli,

Cha tepid aura freschi ognora serba,

Sicuri si vedean lepri e conigli:

E cervi con la fronte alta e superba,

Senza temer che alcun li uccida o pigli,

Pascono, e stansi ruminando l'erba:

E Saltan daini e capri snelli e destri,

Che sono in copia in quei luoghi campestri.

M. de Laval was in raptures with the gardens of Estherhasie. In the height of his admiration, I asked him how they stood in his opinion, compared with those of Versailles?

Ah, Parbleu! Monsieur, answered he, Versailles étoit fait exprès pour n'être comparé à rien.—He acknowledged, however, without difficulty, that, except France, no other country he had seen was so beautiful as this.

Having wandered here many hours, we returned to the inn, where a servant waited with Prince Estherhasie's compliments, and a basket containing two bottles of Tokay, and the same quantity of Champaign and of Old Hock. We lamented very sincerely, that we could not have the honour of waiting on this very magnificent Prince, and thanking him personally for so much politeness.

A company of Italian singers and actors were then at the inn, and preparing for the opera. Great preparations were making for the entertainment of the Empress and all the Court, who are soon to make a visit of several days to Estherhasie. Though the Imperial family, and many of the nobility, are to lodge in the palace, yet every corner of this large and commodious inn is already bespoke for the company which are invited upon that occasion.

Hungary is a very cheap country, the land being infinitely fertile, and in some places producing the most esteemed grape in Europe. It is beautiful with lakes, the windings of the Danube, and many streams which flow into that fine river. In the woods of Hungary are bred a race of horses, the most active, hardy, and spirited, for their size, in the world. These have been found very useful in war, and the hussars, or light dragoons of the Austrian army, are mounted on them.

The men in Hungary are remarkably handsome, and well-shaped. Their appearance is improved by their dress, which you know is peculiar, and very becoming.

Lady M. W. Montague asserts, that the Hungarian women are far more beautiful than the Austrian. For my part, I think of women, as M. de Laval does of Versailles;—that they are not to be compared with any thing,—not even with one another. And therefore, without presuming to take a comparative view of their beauty, it may be remarked in general, that where the men are handsome and well-made, it is natural to suppose, that the women will possess the same advantages; for parents generally bestow as much attention to the making of their daughters as of their sons. In confirmation of which doctrine, I can assure you, that I have seen as handsome women, as men, in Hungary, and one of the prettiest women, in my opinion, at present at the Court of Vienna, is a Hungarian.

None of the Empress's subjects are taxed so gently, or enjoy so many privileges as the Hungarians. This is partly owing to the grateful remembrance she has of their loyalty and attachment in the days of her distress. But although this sentiment were not so strong in her breast as it really is, there are political reasons for continuing to them the same exemptions and privileges; for nothing can be more dangerous than disobliging the inhabitants of a frontier country, which borders on an inveterate enemy.—Nor could any thing please the Turks more, than to find the hearts of the Hungarians alienated from the house of Austria.

I found this country, and the company of M. de Laval, so very agreeable, that I should have been happy to have extended our excursion farther; but he is obliged to set out soon for Chamberry to pay his duty to the Comte d'Artois, who is expected there to wait on his future spouse, the Princess of Savoy. We therefore returned by the direct road from Estherhasie to Vienna.

LETTER LXXXIX.

Vienna.

So the fate of poor —— is finally decided, and he now finds, that to be ruined is not a matter of so much indifference as he once imagined. I neither see the possibility of his extricating himself from his present difficulties, nor in what manner he will be able to support them. Accustomed to every luxuriant indulgence, how can he bear the inconveniencies of poverty?— Dissipated and inattentive from his childhood, how can he make any exertion for himself?—His good-humour, genteel figure, and pliant disposition, made him well received by all.—While he formed no expectations from their friendship, his company seemed particularly acceptable to some who are at present in power: Whether it will be equally so now, when he has nothing else to depend on, is to be tried. And I really think it as well for him that it be tried now, as five or six years hence.

This calamity has been long foreseen.—There seemed to be almost a necessity that it should happen sooner or later; for he had neither caution, plan, nor object in his gaming.—He continued it from habit alone. Of all mankind, he was the least covetous of excessive wealth; and exclusive of gaming, he always lived within his income, not from a desire of saving money, but merely because he had no taste for great expence.—How often have we seen him lose immense sums to those who could never have paid the half, had he happened to win it; and to some of whom he had lent the money which enabled them to stake against him?

There are many careless young men of great fortunes, who game in the same style, and from no other motives than those of our unhappy friend.—What is the consequence?—The money circulates for a while among them, but remains finally with persons of a very different character.—I shall not suppose that any of the very fortunate gamesters we have been acquainted with, have used those means to correct fortune which are generally reckoned fraudulent. I am fully persuaded, they are seldomer practised in the clubs in London, than in any other gaming societies in the world.—Let all slight of hand, and every species of downright sharping, be put out of the question; but still we may suppose, that among a great number of careless inattentive people of fortune, a few wary, cool and shrewd men are mingled, who know how to conceal real caution and design under apparent inattention and gaiety of manner;—who have a perfect command of themselves, push their luck when fortune smiles, and refrain when she changes her disposition;—who have calculated the chances, and understand every game where judgment is required.

If there are such men, is not the probability of winning infinitely in their favour?—Does it not amount to almost as great a certainty, as if they had actually loaded the dice or packed the cards?—I know you live in the habit of intimacy with some who answer to the above description; and I have heard you say, that however fortunate they may have been, you were fully convinced that nothing can be fairer than their manner of playing. I accuse them of taking no other advantages than those above mentioned; but I appeal to your own experience,—pray recollect, and I am greatly mistaken, if you will not find, that by far the greater part of those who have made fortunes by play, and have kept them when made, are men of cool, cautious, shrewd, and selfish characters.

If any of these very fortunate people were brought to a trial, and examined by what means they had accumulated such sums, while so many others had entirely lost, or greatly impaired their fortunes (if the word esprit be allowed to imply that artful superiority which belongs to their characters), they might answer in the words of the wife of Concini Marechal d'Ancre, when she was asked what charm she had made use of to fascinate the mind of the Queen?—De l'ascendant, she replied, qu'un esprit superieur a toujours sur des esprits foibles.—Certainly there can be no greater weakness, than for a man of independent fortune to game in such a manner as to risk losing it, for the chance of doubling or tripling his income: because the additional happiness arising from any supposable addition of wealth, can never be within a thousand degrees so great, as the misery which would be the consequence of his being stripped of his original fortune.

This consideration alone, one would imagine, might be sufficient to deter any reasonable man from a conduct so weak and absurd: yet there are other considerations which give much additional weight to the argument;—the dismal effects which the continued practice of gaming has sometimes been observed to produce in the disposition of the mind, and the most essential parts of the character, destroying every idea of œconomy, engrossing the whole time, undermining the best principles, perverting the qualities of the heart, rendering men callous to the ruin of acquaintances, and partakers, with a savage insensibility, in the spoils of their unwary friends.

The peculiar instances with which you and I are acquainted, where the long-continued habit of deep play has had no such effects, are proofs of the rooted honour and integrity of certain individuals, and may serve as exceptions to a general rule, but cannot be urged as arguments against the usual tendency of gaming. If men of fortune and character adopted the practice of gaming upon any principle of reasoning, there might be a greater probability of their being reasoned out of it: but most of them begin to game, not with any view or fixed plan of increasing their wealth, but merely as a fashionable amusement, or perhaps by way of showing the liberality of their spirit, and their contempt for money.

I would not be very positive, that some of them have not mistaken for admiration that surprise which is expressed when any person has lost an immense sum. And this mistake may have given them less repugnance to the idea of becoming the objects of admiration in the same day. Afterwards endeavouring to win back what they had so idly lost, the habit has grown by degrees, and at length has become their sole resource from the weariness which those born to great fortunes, and who have not early in life acquired some faculty of amusing themselves, are more prone to fall into than others. Men born to no such expectations, whatever their natural dispositions may be, are continually roused from indolence by avocations which admit of no delay. The pursuit of that independence, for which almost every human bosom sighs, and whose value is unknown only to those who have always possessed it, is thought a necessary, and is often sound, an agreeable employment to the generality of mankind. This, with the other duties of life, is sufficient to engross their time and thoughts, and guard them from *the pains and penalties of idleness.*

As the pursuit of wealth is superfluous in men of rank and fortune, so it would be unbecoming their situation. Being deprived of this, which is so great an object and resource to the rest of mankind, they stand in more need of something to supply its place. I know of nothing which can so completely, and with so much propriety, have this effect, as a taste for letters and love of science. I therefore think these are more essentially necessary to the happiness of people of high rank and great fortune, than to those in confined circumstances.

If independence be desired with universal ardour by mankind, the road of science is neither the most certain, nor the shortest way to attain it. But those who are already in possession of this, have infinite need of the other to teach them to enjoy their independence with dignity and satisfaction, and to prevent the gifts of fortune from becoming sources of misery instead of happiness. If they are ambitious, the cultivation of letters, by adorning their minds, and enlarging their faculties, will facilitate their plans, and render them more fit for the high situations to which they aspire. If they are devoid of ambition, they have still more occasion for some of the pursuits of science, as resources against the languor of retired or inactive life.—Quod si non hic tantus fructus ostenderetur, et si ex his studiis delectatio sola peteretur; tamen, ut opinor, hanc animi remissionem, humanissimam ac liberalissimam judicaretis.

This love of letters considered merely as an amusement, and to fill up agreeably the vacant hours of life, I believe to be more essentially necessary to men of great fortune than to those who have none;—to men without ambition, than to those who are animated by that active passion; and to the generality of Englishmen more than to the natives of either Germany or France.—The Germans require very little variety. They can bear the languid uniformity of life always with patience, and often with satisfaction. They display an equanimity under disgust that is quite astonishing.—The French, though not so celebrated for patience, are of all mankind the least liable to despondence. Public affairs, so apt to disturb the repose of many worshipful citizens of London, never give a Frenchman uneasiness. If the arms of France are successful, he rejoices with all his heart;—if they are unfortunate, he laughs at the commanders with all his soul. If his mistress is kind, he celebrates her goodness and commends her taste;—if she is cruel, he derides her folly in the arms of another.

No people ever were so fond of amusement, and so easily amused. It seems to be the chief object of their lives, and they contrive to draw it from a thousand sources, in which no other people ever thought it could be found. I do not know where I met with the following lines; they are natural and easy, and seem expressive of the conduct and sentiments of the whole French nation.

M'amuser n'importe comment,

Fait toute ma philosophie.

Je crois ne perdre aucun moment

Hors le moment où je m'ennuie;

Et je tiens ma tâche finie,

Pourvu qu'ainsi tout doucement;

Je me defasse de la vie.

Our countrymen who have applied to letters, have prosecuted every branch of science as successfully as any of their neighbours. But those of them who study mere amusement, independent of literature of any kind, certainly have not been so happy in their researches as the French. Many things which entertain the latter, seem frivolous and insipid to the former. The English view objects through a darker medium. Less touched than their neighbours with the gaieties, they are more affected by the vexations of life, under which they are too ready to despond. They feel their spirits flag with the repetition of scenes which at first were thought agreeable. This stagnation of animal spirits, from whatever cause it arises, becomes itself a cause of desperate resolutions, and debating habits.

A man of fortune, therefore, who can acquire such a relish for science, as will make him rank its pursuits among his amusements; has thereby made an acquisition of more importance to his happiness, than if he had acquired another estate equal in value to his first. I am almost convinced, that a taste of this kind is the only thing which can render a man of fortune (especially if his fortune be very large) tolerably independent and easy through life. Whichsoever of the roads of science he loves to follow, his curiosity will continually be kept awake. An inexhaustible variety of interesting objects will open to his view,—his mind will be replenished with ideas,—and even when the pursuits of ambition become insipid, he will still have antidotes against tædium, and (other things being supposed equal) the best chance of passing agreeably through life, that the uncertainty of human events allows to man.

LETTER XC.

In your last, you show such a passion for anecdote, and seem so desirous of my insisting on manners and characters, that I fear you will not be pleased with my last long epistle upon a subject entirely remote from what you demand. But you must remember that you were warned from the beginning of this correspondence, that I would retain the privilege of digressing as often as I pleased, and that my letters should frequently treat of what I thought, as well as what I saw. However, this shall consist entirely of sights.

The first I shall mention was exhibited soon after our arrival at Vienna. This was the feast of St. Stephen, at which the Emperor dined in public with the knights.

He was at the head of the table; his brother and brother-in-law next him, and the other knights sat according to seniority. The Arch-duchesses, with some of the principal ladies of the court, were at a balcony within the hall to see this ceremony.—The Emperor and all the knights were dressed in the robes of the order. The Hungarian guards, with their sabres drawn, surrounded the table.

The honour of serving the Emperor at this solemnity belongs entirely to the Hungarians. When he called for drink, a Hungarian nobleman poured a little of the wine into a cup and tasted it; he afterwards filled another, which he presented with one knee touching the ground. The Emperor often smiled upon this nobleman as he went through the ceremony, and seemed to indicate by the whole of his behaviour, that he considered such submissive bendings of one man to another, as greatly misplaced, and that he suffered this mummery merely in compliance with ancient custom.

There was great crowding to see this feast, and it was not without difficulty I got admission; though, after all, there was nothing to be seen but some well-dressed men, who ate an exceeding good dinner with tolerable appetite.

Since the feast of St. Stephen, we have been witnesses to the annual ceremony in commemoration of the defeat of the Turkish army, and the raising the siege of Vienna by John Sobieski king of Poland. The Imperial family and the principal nobility of both sexes walked in solemn procession, and heard mass at the church of St. Stephen on this occasion. In the middle of the street, leading from the palace to the church, a platform was raised, upon which the company, who formed the procession, walked.—The streets were lined with the Imperial guards, and the windows and tops of the houses were crowded with spectators.—The D—— of H—— and I found a very good situation at a window with the Venetian ambassador.

This ceremony would have been too fatiguing for the Empress:—She therefore did not attend:—The Emperor, the Arch-dukes and Duchesses, with all the nobility, did. A prodigious train of bishops, priests, and monks followed; and a numerous band of music played as they went along.

As this is a day of rejoicing, the richest and gayest dresses are thought the most expressive of the pious gratitude becoming such an occasion. The ladies displayed their devotion in the most brilliant manner. Their minds, however, were not so much exalted by heavenly contemplations, as to be above taking notice of their earthly acquaintances at the windows, whom they regaled with smiles and nods as they walked along.

Next day the Imperial family dined in public, and many people went to see them. I was not of the number, though nobody can more sincerely wish them the enjoyment of all the comforts of life. I know not on what principle the Royal Family in France, and other countries in Europe, have adopted the custom of eating in public. They cannot imagine, that the seeing them chew and swallow their victuals can create a vast deal of admiration in the beholders. It would certainly be taken for granted, that they could perform these necessary functions, although a cloud of witnesses were not admitted to confirm the fact. If these exhibitions are designed for the entertainment of the subjects, a thousand could be thought of more amusing to them; for however interesting the part of an actor at a feast may be, that of a spectator is surely one of the most insipid that can be imagined.

But the same evening there was a grand masquerade at Schonbrun, which was more generally amusing.—Four thousand tickets were distributed on this occasion.—A large party of dragoons were placed along the road from Vienna, to keep the coaches in a regular line, and to prevent confusion. The principal rooms of this magnificent palace were thrown open for the reception of the company.—In three large halls on the ground-floor, tables were covered with a cold collation of all kinds of fowls, ham, and confections, with pine-apples and every sort of fruit. These, with Old Hock, Champagne, and other kinds of wine, were served with readiness and profusion to all who asked for them.

At the end of the large dining-room, there was a raised seat for the Empress, and some ladies who attended her. Here a grand Ballet was danced by the Arch-duke, the Arch-duchesses, the Princess of Modena, and some of the chief nobility, to the number of twenty-four. The dancers, both male and female, were dressed in white silk, flounced with pink-coloured ribands, and enriched with a vast profusion of diamonds.

This ballet was performed three times at proper intervals. Those who had seen it once, passed into the gallery, and other apartments, giving way to a new set of spectators. In the garden, on a rising ground opposite to the palace windows, a temporary fabric was erected in the form of a large and magnificent temple. This was illuminated by an incredible number of lamps, and gave the appearance of a very extraordinary piece of architecture, which continued flaming through the whole night, and had a very fine effect, viewed from Vienna, and other places at a greater distance.

The Emperor mixed with the company without ceremony or distinction, taking no part himself but as a spectator. He was conversing in the middle of the hall, in the most familiar manner, with an English gentleman, without observing, that the third ballet was going to be danced, when the master of the ceremonies whispered him in the ear.—The Emperor, seizing the Englishman by the arm, said, Allons, Monsieur, on nous chasse—il faut se retirer; and immediately walked into another room, to give place to others who had not yet seen the dance.

This very splendid entertainment was given to the Arch-duke, and the Princess of Modena, whose usual residence is at Milan.—The Empress, thus surrounded by her offspring, appeared cheerful and happy.—She seemed to enjoy the vivacity, and sympathize with the gaiety, of the company.—She is greatly beloved by her own children, and by her subjects in general, whom she also considers as her children in a greater degree than is usual for sovereigns.

It is an error to imagine, that great devotion has a tendency to sour the temper: Though it must be acknowledged, that it has not always the power of sweetening the very austere trunks on which it is sometimes grafted; but in a character naturally benevolent, every good disposition will be strengthened and animated by real piety. Of this I have seen a thousand instances, and I believe her Imperial Majesty affords one.

LETTER XCI.

The Emperor is of a middle size, well made, and of a fair complexion. He has a considerable resemblance to his sister, the Queen of France, which, in my opinion, is saying a great deal in favour of his looks.—Till I saw something of his usual behaviour, I did not think it possible for a person in such an elevated situation, to put every body with whom he conversed upon so easy a footing.

His manner, as I have often mentioned, is affable, obliging, and perfectly free from the reserved and lofty deportment assumed by some on account of high birth. Whoever has the honour to be in company with him, so far from being checked by such despicable pride, has need to be on his guard, not to adopt such a degree of familiarity as, whatever the condescension of the one might permit, would be highly improper in the other to use.

He is regular in his way of life, moderate in his pleasures, steady in his plans, and diligent in business. He is fond of his army, and inclines that the soldiers should have every comfort and necessary consistent with their situation. He is certainly an œconomist, and lavishes very little money on useless pomp, mistresses, or favourites; and it is, I suppose, on no better foundation than this, that his enemies accuse him of avarice.

I cannot help regarding œconomy as one of the most useful qualities in a Prince. Liberality, even when pushed to an imprudent length, may, in a private person, proceed from a kind of greatness of mind, because his fortune is in every sense his own, and he can injure nobody but himself by lavishing it away.—He knows that when it is gone, nobody will reimburse him for his extravagance.—He seems therefore to have taken the resolution to submit to the inconveniency of future poverty, rather than renounce the present happiness of acting with a magnificent liberality, and bestowing on others more than he can afford.

This is not the case with a Prince.—What he squanders is not his own, but the public money.—He knows that his pomp and splendour will be kept up, and that his subjects, not he, are to feel the inconveniencies of his prodigality. When I hear, therefore, that a King has given great sums of money to any particular person; from the sums given, the person who receives it, the motive for the gift, and other circumstances, I can judge whether it is well or ill disposed of; but in either case, it cannot be called generosity.

The virtue of generosity consists in a man's depriving himself of something for the sake of another. There can be no generosity in giving to John what James must replace the next moment. What is called generosity in Kings, very often consists in bestowing that money on the idle part of their subjects which they have squeezed from the industrious. I have heard a parcel of fiddlers and opera dancers praise a Prince for his noble and generous behaviour to them, while men near his person of useful talents and real worth were distressed for bread.—The Emperor certainly has none of that kind of generosity.

His usual dress (the only one indeed in which I ever saw him, except at the feast of the Knights of St. Stephen) is a plain uniform of white faced with red.—When he goes to Laxenberg, Schonbrun, and other places near Vienna, he generally drives two horses in an open chaise, with a servant behind, and no other attendant of any kind.—He very seldom allows the guard to turn out as he passes through the gate.—Nobody ever had a stronger disposition to judicious inquiry.—He is fond of conversing with ingenious people.—When he hears of any person, of whatever rank or country, being distinguished for any particular talent, he is eager to converse with him, and turns the conversation to the subject on which that person is thought to excel, drawing from him all the useful information he can. Of all the means of knowledge, this is perhaps the most powerful, and the most proper that can be used by one whose more necessary occupations do not leave him much time for study.

He seems to be of opinion, that the vanity and ignorance of many Princes are frequently owing to the forms in which they are intrenched, and to their being deprived of the advantages which the rest of mankind enjoy from a free comparison and exchange of sentiment. He is convinced, that unless a King can contrive to live in some societies on a footing of equality, and can weigh his own merit, without throwing his guards and pomp into the scale, it will be difficult for him to know either the world or himself.

One evening at the Countess Walstein's, the conversation leading that way, the Emperor enumerated some remarkable and ludicrous instances of the inconveniencies of etiquette, which had occurred at a certain court. One person present hinted at the effectual means his Majesty had used to banish every inconveniency of that kind from the Court of Vienna. To which he replied, It would be hard indeed, if, because I have the ill fortune to be an Emperor, I should be deprived of the pleasures of social life, which are so much to my taste. All the grimace and parade to which people in my situation are accustomed from their cradle, have not made me so vain, as to imagine that I am in any essential quality superior to other men; and if I had any tendency to such an opinion, the surest way to get rid of it, is the method I take, of mixing in society, where I have daily occasions of finding myself inferior in talents to those I meet with. Conscious of this, it would afford me no enjoyment to assume airs of a superiority which I feel does not exist. I endeavour therefore to please, and to be pleased; and as much as the inconveniency of my situation will permit, to enjoy the blessings of society like other men, convinced that the man who is secluded from those, and raises himself above friendship, is also raised above happiness, and deprived of the means of acquiring knowledge.

This kind of language is not uncommon with poor philosophers; but I imagine it is rarely held by Princes, and the inferences to be drawn from it more rarely put in practice.

A few days after this, there was an exhibition of fire-works on the Prater. This is a large park, planted with wood, and surrounded by the Danube, over which there is a wooden bridge. No carriages being allowed to pass, the company leave their coaches at one end, and walk. There is a narrow path railed off on one side of the bridge. Many people very injudiciously took this path, to which there is an easy entrance at one end, but the exit is difficult at the other; for only one person can go out at a time. The path therefore was very soon choaked up; the unfortunate passengers crept on at a snail's pace, and in the most straitened and disagreeable manner imaginable; whilst those who had kept the wide path in the middle of the bridge, like the fortunate and wealthy in their journey through life, moved along at their ease, totally regardless of the wretched circumstances of their fellow-passengers.

Some few of the prisoners in the narrow passage, who were of a small size, and uncommon address, crawled under the rail, and got into the broad walk in the middle; but all who were tall, and of a larger make, were obliged to remain and submit to their fate. An Englishman, who had been at the Countess Walstein's when the Emperor expressed himself as above mentioned, was of the last class. The Emperor, as he passed, seeing that those of a small size extricated themselves, while the Englishman remained fixed in a very aukward situation, called out, Ah, Monsieur! Je vous ai bien annoncé combien il est incommode d'être trop *grand*.—A present vous devez être bien de mon avis;—Mais comme je ne puis rien faire pour vous soulager, je vous recommende à Saint George.

There are people who, having heard of the Emperor's uncommon affability, and of his total contempt of pomp and parade, of which the bulk of mankind are so much enamoured, have asserted, that the whole is affectation. But if the whole tenor of any person's words and actions is to be considered as affectation, I do not know by what means we are to get at the bottom of his real character. Yet, people who have a violent taste for any particular thing, are extremely ready to believe, that those who have not the same taste are affected.

I do not remember that I ever told you, that our friend R———, who loves his bottle above all things, and who, I believe, esteems you above all men, let me into a part of your character of which I never had the smallest suspicion.

One day after dinner, when a couple of bottles had awakened his friendship, and laid open his heart, he took it into his head to enumerate your good qualities, and concluded the list, by saying, that you were no milk-sop.—I know what that expression imports in the mouth of R———. I therefore stared, and said, I had seldom seen you drink above three glasses at a time in my life.—Nor I, said he; but take my word for it, he is too honest a fellow not to love good wine, and I am certain his sobriety is all affectation.

LETTER XCII.

I returned very lately from Prince Lichtenstein's house at Felberg in Austria, where I passed a few days very agreeably. The Lichtenstein family is one of the first in this country, whether considered in point of antiquity, wealth or dignity. This Prince, besides his lands in Austria, has considerable estates in Bohemia, Moravia, and that part of Silesia which belongs to the Empress. Like Prince Estherhasie, he has body-guards in his own pay.—I believe no other subjects in Europe retain this distinction.

Felberg is a fine old mansion, about forty miles from Vienna. The apartments are large, convenient, and furnished in the magnificent style which prevails in the noblemen's houses of this country. The company consisted of the Prince and Princess, the Count Degenfeldt and his Lady, a very accomplished woman; the D—— of H——, Mr. M——, an English officer, another English gentleman, and myself. Our entertainment was in every respect splendid, particularly in the article of attendants. Some of the Austrian nobility carry this point of magnificence to a height, which could scarcely be supported by the best estates in England, where one footman is more expensive than four in this country.

The day after our arrival, breakfast was served to the company separately in their own apartments, as is the custom here. We afterwards set out for another villa belonging to this Prince, at six miles distance, where he intended to give the D—— the amusement of hunting. The Princess, the Countess Degenfeldt, the D——, and Captain M——, were in one coach; the Prince, the Count, and I, in another; the two young Princes, with their governor and the young English gentleman, in a third, with a great retinue on horseback.

As the day was well advanced when we arrived, I imagined the hunting would begin immediately:—But every thing is done with method and good order in this country, and it was judged proper to dine in the first place. This in due time being concluded, I thought the men would have proceeded directly to the scene of action, leaving the ladies till their return.—But here I found myself again mistaken:—The ladies were to assist in the whole of this expedition. But as there was a necessity to traverse a large wood, into which coaches could not enter, vehicles of a more commodious construction were prepared. I forget what name is given to these carriages. They are of the form of benches, with stuffed seats, upon which six or eight people may place themselves one behind the other. They are drawn by four horses, and slide over the ground like a sledge, passing along paths and trackless ways, over which no wheel-carriage could be drawn.

After being conveyed in this manner across the wood, and a considerable way beyond it, we came to a very large open field, in which there were several little circular inclosures of trees and underwood at wide intervals from each other.—This hunting had hitherto been attended with very little fatigue; for we had been carried the whole way in coaches, or on the sledges, which are still easier than any coach. In short, we had been perfectly passive since breakfast, except during the time of dinner.

But when we arrived at this large plain, I was informed, that the hunting would commence within a very short time. I then expected we should have some violent exercise after so much inactivity, and began to fear that the ladies might be over-fatigued, when, lo! the Prince's servants began to arrange some portable chairs at a small distance from one of the thickets above mentioned. The Princess, Countess, and the rest of the company took their places; and when every body was seated, they assured me that the hunting was just going to begin.

I own, my curiosity was now excited in a very uncommon degree; and I was filled with impatience to see the issue of a hunting, which had been conducted in a style so different from any idea I had of that diversion. While I sat lost in conjecture, I perceived, at a great distance, a long line of people moving towards the little wood, near which the company was seated. As they walked along, they gradually formed the segment of a circle, whose centre was this wood. I understood that these were peasants, with their wives and children, who, walking forward in this manner, rouse the game, which naturally take shelter in the thicket of trees and bushes. As soon as this happened, the peasants rushed in at the side opposite to that where our company had taken post, beat out the game, and then the massacre began.

Each person was provided with a fusil, and many more were at hand loaded for immediate use. The servants were employed in charging as fast as the pieces were fired off: So that an uninterrupted shooting was kept up, as long as the game continued flying or running out of the wood—The Prince hardly ever missed.—He himself killed above thirty partridges, a few pheasants, and three hares.

At the beginning of this scene, I was a good deal surprised to see a servant hand a fusil to the Princess, who with great coolness, and without rising from her seat, took aim at a partridge, which immediately fell to the ground. With the same ease, she killed ten or twelve partridges and pheasants, at about double the number of shots.—The execution done by the rest of the company was by no means considerable.

Though I had not heard of it before, I now understood, that shooting is not an uncommon amusement with the German ladies: And it is probable, their attention to the delicacy of the fair sex, has induced the hardy Germans to render this diversion so little fatiguing.

The company afterwards walked to other little inclosures of planting, where some game was driven out and killed as before.—The following day, the Prince conducted us to another of his seats, where there is a very fine open wood, full of deer of every kind, some of them the largest I ever saw. There is also a great number of wild boars, one of which, by the Prince's permission, the D—— of H—— killed.

Nothing could surpass the politeness and magnificence with which the company were entertained during the whole of their stay. The Princess is a woman of an amiable character, and a good understanding; educates her children, and manages her affairs with the utmost prudence and propriety.

This family, and many of the nobility, who have hitherto been at their country-seats, are now about to return to Vienna. The family of Monsieur and Madame de Pergen have been here for some time. This lady is an intimate friend of the Countess Thune; and nearly the same company, who form her society, now assemble twice a week at the house of Madame de Pergen, who rivals the Countess in good sense and many accomplishments, and, without raising jealousy or ill-will, divides with her the esteem of the best company of this place. The agreeable footing on which society is established here, and the number of respectable people with whom we are acquainted, fills me with regret at the thoughts of leaving Vienna; but the D—— of H—— inclines to pass the winter in Italy. Indeed, if he did not, he would be obliged to delay the journey a whole year, or submit to the inconveniencies of travelling in the summer months, which, in so hot a climate, is rather to be avoided.

LETTER XCIII.

I have not said any thing of the Austrian army, having some suspicion that I rather over-dosed you with military details from Berlin, where the subject of my letters was continually before my eyes. But the Emperor has very few of his troops in garrison at Vienna. They make a fine appearance, and the army in general are more judiciously clothed, than any other I have seen.

Instead of coats with long skirts, their uniform is a short jacket of white cloth, with waistcoat and breeches of the same, and each soldier has a surtout of coarse gray cloth, which he wears in cold or rainy weather. This he rolls up in a very small bulk when the weather is good, and it is little or no incumbrance on a march. They have short boots for shoes; and, in place of hats, they wear caps of very stout leather, with a brass front, which usually stands up, but which may be let down upon occasion, to prevent their eyes from being incommoded by the sun.

Except a very few Hungarians who do duty within the palace, there are no troops in the Austrian service with increased pay, and exclusive privileges, under the denomination of body-guards; the marching regiments on the ordinary establishment, form the garrison of Vienna, and perform the duty of guards by rotation.

The insolence of the Prætorian bands at Rome, so often terrible to their masters; the frequent insurrections of the Janissaries at Constantinople, and the revolutions effected by the Russian guards, at Petersburgh, sufficiently point out the danger of such an institution. These examples may have influenced the Austrian government to renounce a system which seems to render certain regiments less useful, and more dangerous, than the rest of the army.

The Austrian army is calculated at considerably above two hundred thousand; and, it is imagined, that there never was a greater number of excellent officers in the service than at present; so that in case of a war with Prussia, the two powers will be more equally matched than ever. It would be unfortunate for this Court if it should break out at present, for there are some commotions among the peasants in Bohemia, which occasion a general disquiet, and by which some individuals have sustained great losses. One nobleman of the first rank has had his house, and all the furniture, burnt to the ground, together with some large out-houses near his castle.

These excesses, according to some, proceed from mere wantonness, and love of mischief, in the people. Others assert, that they are excited by the tyranny of the lords, which has driven those poor men to despair. Whichsoever of these accounts is true, it seems evident to me, that it would be much better for the lords, as well as the peasants, that the latter, instead of being bond-men, were in a state of freedom. At present, they pay their rent by working a certain number of days in the week for their masters, and maintain themselves and families by labouring the other days on their own account. You will readily believe, that more real business will be done in one day when they work for themselves, than in two days labour for their lords. This occasions ill-humour and blows on the part of the master, and hatred and revolt on that of the peasants.

If the estates in Bohemia were let to free-men at a reasonable rent, freedom and property would excite a spirit of industry among these indolent people. They would then work every day with cheerfulness and good-will, and I am convinced the landlords revenues would increase daily. In consequence of this, the peasants would, in all probability, continue as much attached to the ground from choice, as they are at present from necessity.—Do we not see families in Great Britain remain for many generations on gentlemen's estates, though the master has the privilege of changing his tenant, and the tenant his master, at the end of every lease?

In almost every country in Europe, except England, the inhabitants are confined by some barrier or other, to the situation in which they are born. The total want of education necessarily obliges the greater part to gain their livelihood by bodily labour. National opinions prevent others from ever rising above the level of their birth, however sublime their genius, or however great their acquired knowledge. But in our island the door of science, and consequently the road to ambition, is open to almost every individual. Even in the most remote villages some degree of education is bestowed on the poorest inhabitants.

This may be of little or no importance to ninety-nine in a hundred; and if the small number who, by improving this pittance of knowledge, raise themselves above the state in which they were born, very few arrive at any degree of eminence; the reason of which is, that great genius is a quality very sparingly dealt out to mankind. Though it must be allowed, that much the greater part of the inhabitants of the same country and climate are born with nearly the same natural abilities; and that the degrees of education, and other opportunities of improvement, gradually form all the difference which appears among them in after-life; yet I cannot, with Helvetius, believe that genius is entirely the work of education.

I am fully convinced, that Nature is continually producing some individuals in every nation of a finer organization, with an infinitely greater aptitude for science of every kind, and whose minds are capable of a more sublime and extensive range of thought, than is attainable by the common run of mankind with any possible degree of culture. This natural superiority is what I call genius. Wherever a considerable share of this is lodged, a little cultivation will be sufficient, but some is absolutely requisite to make it appear.

When it does exist in the minds of peasants in Russia, Poland, and some parts of Germany, it remains dormant from neglect, or is smothered by oppression. But in Great Britain, the degree of education which is now universal, small as it is, will be sufficient to rouse, animate, and bring into action the fire of extraordinary genius, the seeds of which impartial Nature is as apt to place in the infant breast of a peasant as of a prince. The chance of great and distinguished men springing up in a country, is therefore not to be calculated by the number of inhabitants, but by the number whose minds receive that degree of cultivation necessary to call forth their latent powers.

On the supposition, that one kingdom contains eight millions of inhabitants, and another triple the number, many more men of original genius, and great eminence in every art and science, may, from the circumstances above mentioned, be expected to appear in the first than in the second. In Great Britain, for example, almost all the natives may be included in the calculation; but in the other countries which I have mentioned, the peasantry, who form the most numerous class, must be struck out.

LETTER XCIV.

Whether it is owing to the example of the Empress, or to what other cause, I shall not take upon me to decide; but there certainly appears a warmer and more general attachment to religion in Vienna, than in any other great town in Germany: There is also a greater appearance of satisfaction and happiness here than in many other cities, where religious impressions are more feeble and, less prevalent: It is not improbable, that the latter may be a consequence of the former.

Irreligion and scepticism, exclusive of the bad effects they may have on the morals or future destiny of men, impair even their temporal happiness, by obscuring those hopes, which, in some situations, are their only consolation. In whatever superior point of view those men may consider themselves, who deride the opinions which their fellow-citizens hold sacred, this vanity is often overbalanced by the irksome doubts which obtrude on their minds. Uncertainty with respect to the most interesting of all subjects, or a fixed persuasion of annihilation, are equally insupportable to the greater part of mankind, who sooner or later endeavour to put in a claim for that bright reversion, which religion has promised to believers. If the idea of annihilation has been supported without pain by a few philosophers, it is the utmost that can be said; such a state of mind can never be a source of satisfaction or pleasure. People of great sensibility seldom endure it long; their fond desire of immortality overturns every fabric which scepticism had attempted to raise in their minds; they cannot abide by a doctrine which plucks from the heart a deeply-rooted hope, tears asunder all those ties of humanity, affection, friendship, and love, which it has been the business of their lives to bind, and which they expect will be eternal. Since sensibility renders the heart averse to scepticism, and inclinable to devotion, we may naturally expect to find women more devout than men; very few of that delicate sex have been able to look with stedfast eyes on a prospect, which terminates in a dismal blank; and those few, who have had that degree of philosophical fortitude, have not been the most amiable of the sex.

None of my female acquaintance at Vienna are in this uncomfortable state of mind, but many of them have embroidered some fanciful piece of superstition of their own upon the extensive ground which the Roman Catholic faith affords. In a lady's house a few days ago I happened to take up a book which lay upon the table,—a small picture of the Virgin Mary on vellum fell from between the leaves; under the figure of the Virgin there was an inscription, which I translate literally:

"This is presented by ―― ―― to her dearest friend ―― ――, in token of the sincerest regard and affection; begging that as often as she beholds this figure of the blessed Virgin, she may mix a sentiment of affection for her absent friend, with the emotions of gratitude and adoration she feels for the Mother of Jesus."

The lady informed me, that it was usual for intimate friends to send such presents to each other when they were about to separate, and when there was a probability of their being long asunder.

There seems to be something exceedingly tender and pathetic in blending friendship with religious sentiments, and thus by a kind of consecration endeavouring to preserve the former from the effects of time and absence.— The perusal of this inscription recalled to my memory certain connections I have at home, the impetuosity of which recollection affected me beyond expression.

I remarked in this lady's house another beautiful picture of the Virgin, ornamented with a rich frame, and a silk curtain to preserve it from dust; I observed that she never looked at it but with an air of veneration and love, nor passed it when uncovered by the curtain without a gentle bending of the knee.—She told me, that this picture had been long in the family, and had been always held in the highest esteem, for that both her mother and she owed some of the most fortunate events of their lives to the protection of the blessed Virgin, and she seemed not intirely free from a persuasion that the attention of the Virgin was in some degree retained by the good offices of this identical picture. She declared that the confidence she had in the Virgin's goodness and protection, was one of the greatest comforts she had in life—that to *her* she could, without restraint, open her heart, and pour out her whole soul under every affliction, and she never failed to find herself comforted and relieved by such effusions.

I observed, that devout Protestants found the same consolation in addressing the Almighty.

She said—She could not comprehend how that could be—for that God the Father was so great and awful, that her veneration was mixed with such a degree of dread as confounded all her ideas when she attempted to approach him; but the blessed Mary was of so mild, so condescending, and compassionate a character, that she could address her with more confidence.

She said, she knew it was her duty to adore the Creator of the universe, and she fulfilled it to the best of her power, but she could not divest herself of a certain degree of restraint in her devotions to him, or even to her Saviour; but the blessed Mary being herself a woman, and acquainted with all the weakness and delicacies of the sex, she could to *her* open her heart with a degree of freedom which it was not possible for her to use to any of the Persons of the Holy Trinity.—Regardez sa physionomie, added she, pointing to the picture,—mon Dieu, qu'elle est douce, qu'elle est gracieuse!

These sentiments, however contrary to the Protestant tenets, and the maxims of philosophy, are not unnatural to the human heart.—Voltaire says, that man has always shewn an inclination to create God after his own image; this lady formed an idea of the blessed Virgin from the representation of the painter, as well as from the account given of her in the Evangelists; and her religion allowing the Mother of Christ to be an object of worship, she naturally turned the ardor of her devotion to her whose power she imagined was sufficient to protect her votaries here, and procure them paradise hereafter, and whose character she thought in some particulars sympathised with her own.

Some zealous Protestants may possibly be shocked at this lady's theological notions; however, as in other respects she is a woman of an excellent character, and observes the moral precepts of Christianity with as much attention as if her creed had been purified by Luther, and doubly refined by Calvin, it is hoped they will not think it too great an extension of charity to suppose that her speculative errors may be forgiven.

LETTER XCV.

Vienna.

The preference which is given by individuals in Roman Catholic countries to particular Saints, proceeds sometimes from a supposed connection between the characters of the Saints and the votaries; men expect the greatest favour and indulgence from those who most resemble themselves, and naturally admire others for the qualities which they value most in their own character.

A French Officer of dragoons, being at Rome, went to view the famous statue of Moses by Michael Angelo; the artist has conveyed into this master-piece, in the opinion of some, all the dignity which a human form and human features are capable of receiving; he has endeavoured to give this statue a countenance worthy of the great legislator of the Jews, the favourite of Heaven, who had conversed face to face with the Deity. The officer happened to be acquainted with the history of Moses, but he laid no great stress on any of these circumstances—he admired him much more on account of one adventure in which he imagined Moses had acquitted himself like a man of spirit, and as he himself would have done—Voilà qui est terrible! voilà qui est sublime! cried he at sight of the statue—and after a little pause he added, on voit là un drôle qui a donné des coups de bâton en son tems, et qui a tué son homme.

The crucifixes, and statues, and pictures, of Saints, with which Popish churches are filled, were no doubt intended to awaken devotion when it became drowsy, and to excite in the mind gratitude and veneration for the holy persons they represent; but it cannot be denied that the gross imaginations of the generality of mankind are exceedingly prone to forget the originals, and transfer their adoration to the senseless figures which they behold, and before which they kneel. So that whatever was the original design, and whatever effects those statues and pictures have on the minds of calm, sensible Roman Catholics, it is certain that they often are the objects of as complete idolatry as ever was practised in Athens or Rome, before the statues of Jupiter or Apollo.

On what other principle do such multitudes flock from all the Roman Catholic countries in Europe to the shrine of our Lady at Loretto? Any statue of the Virgin would serve as effectually as that to recall her to the memory, and people may adore her as devoutly in their own parish churches, as in the chapel at Loretto.—The pilgrims therefore must be persuaded that there is some divine influence or intelligence in the statue which is kept there; that it has a consciousness of all the trouble they have taken, and the inconveniencies to which they have been exposed, by long journies, for the sole purpose of kneeling before it in preference to all other images.

It was probably on account of this tendency of the human mind, that the Jews were forbid to make unto themselves any graven image. This indeed seems to have been the only method of securing that superstitious people from idolatry; and notwithstanding the peremptory tenor of the commandment, neither the zeal nor remonstrances of their judges and prophets could always prevent their making idols, nor hinder their worshipping them wherever they found them ready made.

Statues and pictures of Saints which have been long in particular families, are generally kept with great care and attention; the proprietors often have the same kind of attachment to them that the ancient heathens had to their Dii Penates.—They are considered as tutelary and domestic divinities, from whom the family expect protection. When a series of unfortunate events happens in a family, it sometimes creates a suspicion that the family statues have lost their influence. This also is a very ancient sentiment; Suetonius informs us, that the fleet of Augustus having been dispersed by a storm, and many of the ships lost, the Emperor gave orders that the statue of Neptune should not be carried in procession with those of the other Gods, from an opinion that the God of the Sea was unwilling or unable to protect his navy, and in either case he deemed him not worthy of any public mark of distinction.

The genuine tenets of the Roman Catholic church certainly do not authorise any of the superstitions above mentioned, which are generally confined to the credulous and illiterate in the lower ranks of life.—Yet instances are sometimes to be met with in a higher sphere: a Frenchman in a creditable way of life had a small figure of our Saviour on the Cross, of very curious workmanship; he offered it for sale to an English gentleman of my acquaintance; after expatiating on the excellency of the workmanship, he told him that he had long kept this crucifix with the most pious care, that he had always addressed it in his private devotion, and that in return he had expected some degree of protection and favour; instead of which he had of late been remarkably unfortunate; that all the tickets he had in the lottery had proved blanks; and having had a great share in the cargo of a ship coming from the West-Indies, he had recommended it in the most fervent manner in his prayers to the crucifix, and that he might give no offence, by any appearance of want of faith, he had not insured the goods—notwithstanding all which the vessel had been shipwrecked, and the cargo totally lost, though the sailors, in whose preservation he had no concern, had been all saved—Enfin, Monsieur, cried he, with an accent of indignation mingled with regret, and raising his shoulders above his ears, Enfin, Monsieur, il m'a manqué, et je vends mon Christ.

Happy for Christians of every denomination, could they abide by the plain, rational, benevolent precepts of the Christian religion, rejecting all the conceits of superstition, which never fail to deform its original beauty, and to corrupt its intrinsic purity!

LETTER XCVI.

Vienna.

Our disputes with the colonies have been a prevailing topic of conversation wherever we have been since we left England. The warmth with which this subject is handled increases every day.—At present the inhabitants of the continent seem as impatient as those of Great Britain, for news from the other side of the Atlantic, but with this difference, that here they are all of one mind:—all praying for success to the Americans, and rejoicing in every piece of bad fortune which happens to our army.

That the French should be pleased with commotions which must distress and weaken Great Britain, and may transfer to them an equal right to every advantage we gained by the last war, is not surprising; but why the inhabitants of every other country should take part against England, and become partizans of America, is not so apparent.

I should forgive them, and even join in sentiment with them, as far as my regard for the honour and happiness of my country would permit, if this proceeded from an attachment to liberty, and a generous partiality for men who repel oppression, and struggle for independency.—But this is not the case.—Those who can reap no possible advantage from the revolt of America; those who have not an idea of civil liberty, and would even be sorry to see it established in their own country; those who have no other knowledge of the dispute, than that it is ruining England; all join as allies to the Americans, not from love to them, but evidently from dislike to us.

When I first observed this hostile disposition, I thought it might proceed from their being offended at that preference which the English give to their own country and countrymen, above all others: but this conceit we have in common with every other nation on the globe, all of whom cherish the same favourable opinion of themselves. It assuredly prevails in France in an eminent degree.—There is hardly one sceptic or unbeliever in the whole nation.—It is the universal creed, that France is the finest country in the world; the French the most ingenious and most amiable people, excelling in all the arts of peace and war; and that Paris is the capital of politeness, and the center of learning, genius, and taste.

This satisfaction at the misfortunes of Great Britain cannot therefore arise from a cause which is applicable to every other country. It may, indeed, in some measure, proceed from envy of the riches, and jealousy of the power of the English nation; but, I believe, still more from our taking no trouble to conciliate the affections of foreigners, and to diminish that envy and ill-will which great prosperity often creates. The French, though perhaps the vainest people on earth of their own advantages, have some degree of consideration for the feelings and self-love of their neighbours. A Frenchman endeavours to draw from them an acknowledgment of the superiority of his country, by making an elogium on whatever is excellent in theirs. But we are apt to build our panegyric of Old England, on the ruin and wretchedness of all other countries.—Italy is too hot, the inns miserable, and the whole country swarms with monks and other vermin.—In France, the people are slaves and coxcombs, the music execrable;—they boil their meat to rags, and there is no porter, and very little strong ale, in the country.—In Germany, some of their Princes have little more to spend than an English gentleman:—They use stoves instead of grates:—They eat sour crout, and speak High Dutch.— The Danes and Swedes are reminded, that they are rather at too great a distance from the equator; and many sly hints are given concerning the inconveniencies of a cold climate.—Of all things, I should think it most prudent to be silent on this last topic, as so many paltry states will take precedency of Old England, whenever it is the established etiquette that rank shall be determined by climate.

But this consideration has no effect on my honest friend John Bull. When he is in a choleric humour, he will not spare his best friends and nearest neighbours, even when he has most need of their assistance, and when those at a distance seem to have plotted his ruin.—If his own sister Peg should show a disposition to forget old squabbles, to live in friendship with her brother, and should declare that all who renounced his friendship were her enemies, and resolve to conquer by his side, or if that should fail, to die hard along with him—No! d—n ye, says John, none of your coaxing:—You be d—d! you are farther North than I—Keep your distance.—And so he falls a pelting Peg with her own snow-balls; and then turning from her, he attacks Lewis Baboon, Lord Strut, Lord Peter, and dashes their soup maigre, olio's, and maccaroni, full in their teeth.

But to drop allegory; the universal satisfaction which appears all over Europe, at the idea of England's being stript of her colonies, certainly does not intirely originate from political sentiments; but in a great degree from that reserve which keeps Englishmen from cultivating the friendship of foreigners; that pride which hinders them from stooping to humour prejudices; that indifference which makes them disregard the approbation of others, and betray the contempt they are too ready to entertain for customs or sentiments different from their own.

These are things not easily forgiven, and for which no superiority of genius, magnanimity, or integrity, can compensate. The same causes which have made foreigners take part against us in the dispute with America, induce those of them who are rich, and can spend their revenues out of their own country, to prefer France to England for that purpose. The difference between London and Paris in point of climate is very small. The winter amusements of the former are more magnificent; and perhaps every conveniency, and most of the luxuries of life are to be found there in greater perfection. During the summer months, by superior skill in agriculture and a better taste in gardening, England displays such scenes of cultivation, of verdure and fertility, as no country on earth can equal. To these are added the blessings of liberty; yet few or no foreigners reside in England, except those she maintains entirely at her own expence; all the wealthy, after a short visit to London, returning to spend their fortunes at Paris.

Exclusive of pecuniary advantages, it flatters the natural vanity of the French to find their society preferred to that of all other people, and particularly to that of their proud rivals.—Let them enjoy this advantage; let them draw to their capital the idle, the dissipated, and the effeminate of every country in Europe:—but for heaven's sake, do you and your friends in parliament fall on some measure to prevent them from engaging the affections of our industrious brethren of America.

Such an event would be attended with severe consequences to Great Britain, and probably to America. There are, however, so many repelling points in the American and French characters, that I cannot imagine the adhesion between them could be of long duration, should it take place.

You may naturally suppose, from some things in this letter, that the people here are in a particular manner inveterate against England, in her dispute with America. But in reality this is not the case: for although in general they favour America, I have not seen so much moderation on that question any where as at Vienna. The Emperor, when some person asked which side he favoured, replied very ingeniously, Je suis par métier royaliste.

I wish those of our countrymen, who by your account seem to be carrying their zeal for America too far, would remember qu'ils font par naisance Anglois.

Just as I was concluding the above I received yours, informing me that your young friend was in a short time to set out on the usual tour through Europe. I shall take another opportunity of writing to him on the subject you desire, at present I must confine myself to the few following hints.

I hope he will always remember that virtue and good sense are not confined to any particular place, and that one end of travelling is to free the mind from vulgar prejudices—he ought therefore to form connections, and live on a social footing with the inhabitants of the different countries through which he passes; let him at least seem pleased while he remains among them; this is the most effectual method of making them pleased with him, and of his accomplishing every object he can have in visiting their country.

There are instances of Englishmen, who, while on their travels, shock foreigners by an ostentatious preference of England to all the rest of the world, and ridicule the manners, customs, and opinions of every other nation, yet on their return to their own country, immediately assume foreign manners, and continue during the remainder of their lives to express the highest contempt for every thing that is English.—— I hope he will entirely avoid such perverse and ridiculous affectation.

The taste for letters which he has acquired at the university, I dare say will not be diminished on classic ground, or his mind be diverted, by a frivolous enthusiasm for music, or any other passion, from the manly studies and pursuits which become an English gentleman.

As he regards the confidence of his friends, the preservation of his character, and the tranquillity of his mind, let no example, however high, lead him into the practice of deep play. By avoiding gaming he will secure one kind of independence, and at the same time keep possession of another, by continuing the habit of study, till the acquisition of knowledge has become one of his most pleasing amusements.—Unlike those wretched mortals, who, to drag through the dreary hours of life, are continually obliged to have recourse to the assistance of others, this fortunate turn of mind will add to his own happiness, while it renders him more useful to, and less dependent on, society.

The preceding sermon, if you think proper, you may deliver to the young traveller, with my best wishes.

Having delayed our journey several weeks longer than was intended, merely from a reluctance of leaving a place which we have found so very agreeable, we have at length determined to set out for Italy—and are to go by the Duchies of Stiria and Carinthia, which is a shorter route than that by the Tirol. As the time we are to remain at Vienna will be entirely employed in the necessary arrangements for the journey, and the painful ceremony of taking leave of friends, you will not hear again from me till we arrive at Venice.— Mean while, I am, &c.